POST TRAUMATIC SLAVE SYNDROME

Ultimate Guide to Black Mental Health, Generational Trauma, and America's Legacy of Oppression. Find Healing, Resilience, and the Care You Deserve

By Dr. Elara Morgan

Table of Contents

Overview

Post Traumatic Slave Syndrome

PTSS

Overview

Post Traumatic Slave Syndrome PTSS

Post Traumatic Slave Syndrome (PTSS) is a powerful framework that explains how the historical trauma of slavery continues to impact African-descended communities today. PTSS sheds light on how centuries of oppression, forced labor, and systemic racism have left a deep imprint on psychological, emotional, and social well-being. Though slavery ended long ago, its effects did not simply disappear; instead, they evolved into patterns of generational trauma, economic hardship, and cultural disconnection that still affect individuals and communities today.

One of the most significant aspects of PTSS is its effect on mental health. Generations of racial violence, forced assimilation, and socioeconomic exclusion have contributed to widespread anxiety, depression, and chronic stress. The biological imprint of trauma, as explored through epigenetics, suggests that the suffering endured by enslaved ancestors has left lasting changes in DNA, predisposing future generations to heightened stress responses and emotional distress. This inherited trauma can manifest in everyday life as feelings of fear, mistrust, and hopelessness.

PTSS also disrupts family structures and parenting models. Enslaved families were frequently separated, and strict disciplinary measures were often necessary for survival. Over time, these survival-based behaviors became ingrained in family dynamics, leading to patterns of emotional detachment, harsh discipline, and difficulties in expressing vulnerability. Many individuals raised in these environments struggle to break these cycles, further perpetuating emotional and relational challenges.

The economic consequences of PTSS are profound. Generations of denied access to wealth-building opportunities have created systemic financial instability. From slavery to segregation and discriminatory policies such as redlining, African-descended communities have been deliberately excluded from economic advancement. This has contributed to what can be described as financial PTSD, an inherited sense of financial insecurity, risk aversion, and distrust in financial institutions. Break free from these economic barriers requires intentional strategies to rebuild financial literacy, create generational wealth, and challenge economic injustices.

Another major component of PTSS is the internalization of oppression. Centuries of racial dehumanization and cultural erasure have led to an identity crisis among many African-descended individuals. Negative stereotypes, systemic racism, and cultural marginalization have contributed to self-doubt and struggles with self-worth. Many have been conditioned to assimilate into dominant societal norms, often at the expense of their own cultural identity. This ongoing battle between authenticity and societal acceptance creates internal conflicts that can hinder personal and collective growth.

In addition to emotional and economic struggles, PTSS also manifests in physical health issues. Poor diet, addiction, and chronic illnesses such as hypertension and diabetes are prevalent in many Black communities. These health disparities are not accidental but rather the result of limited access to healthcare, food deserts, and generations of unaddressed trauma. The coping mechanisms developed in response to ongoing oppression, such as substance abuse, overeating, and neglecting medical care, can be viewed as forms of low-key self-destruction, further perpetuating cycles of suffering.

Despite these challenges, healing from PTSS is possible. Reclaiming mental health, rebuilding community connections, and embracing cultural heritage are crucial steps toward recovery. Exploring Black identity in a meaningful way, engaging in therapy without stigma, and leveraging spiritual and community-based resources can help individuals and families break free from the grip of inherited trauma. Education, financial empowerment, and proactive self-care are all essential in reclaiming a life of purpose, resilience, and self-determination.

You will come to know in this book, PTSS is not merely a historical reflection, it is a present-day reality that requires acknowledgment and action. By understanding its roots, recognizing its effects, and actively seeking healing, individuals and communities can move beyond generational pain and build a future grounded in strength, empowerment, and self-awareness. The journey toward healing is not easy, but it is necessary to reclaim the dignity, prosperity, and well-being that every person deserves.

Chapter 1

The Psychological Crisis Is Real

CHAPTER 1

The Psychological Crisis Is Real

Let's Fight for Our Sanity Together

For centuries, people of African descent have been subjected to unimaginable trauma, the effects of which reverberate through generations. This is not just history, it's a living reality. It's easy to overlook the toll slavery, colonialism, and systemic racism have taken on the mental well-being of Black individuals, but the psychological scars are deep, persistent, and profound. The psychological crisis is real, and it is not simply a matter of personal hardship but one of collective survival. It's time we confront the weight of this trauma and fight for our sanity together, because the stakes are too high.

The Trauma of Slavery: More Than a Past

The legacy of slavery is not a distant, disconnected event in history, it is an ongoing experience. The trauma of being forcibly removed from your homeland, dehumanized, and treated as property is not something that can be easily erased. It is etched into the very fabric of Black life today. Every generation inherits its ancestors' experiences, and the pain of slavery remains embedded in our collective consciousness.

However, this is not just an emotional or psychological residue. There is mounting evidence that trauma leaves biological imprints on the body, what we now understand as epigenetics. The anguish, fear, and violence endured by ancestors don't simply fade away over time; they are biologically encoded, passed down, influencing the way the brain develops, how the body responds to stress, and even how one's mental health is shaped. This is why many of us feel a sense of inherited sorrow, a burden we cannot always explain but cannot escape. It's a fight that started long before we were born, and for many of us, it continues to be our fight.

The Price of Psychological Disconnection

The cost of this trauma is high. It manifests in different ways, anxiety, depression, addiction, PTSD, and even physical illnesses. The pain caused by slavery doesn't just exist in the past; it lives in us. But unlike physical wounds, the psychological damage is often invisible. We see the aftermath in broken families, fractured communities, and the weight of distrust in institutions meant to help, like healthcare and mental health systems. The legacy of not being able to be "whole" is passed on through generations, leaving emotional fragmentation in its wake.

The emotional toll of slavery is intertwined with everyday experiences of racism, marginalization, and discrimination. Overt acts of violence and microaggressions are one of the daily assaults that take their toll. For many, the constant state of alertness, the need to always be "on guard," creates an emotional exhaustion that is draining. This isn't just about being tired from work or everyday struggles, it's a deep, psychological weariness that affects the mind, body, and spirit.

Unpacking the Weight of Internalized Oppression

One of the most insidious forms of psychological trauma is internalized oppression. This happens when the victim of systemic abuse starts to accept the negative stereotypes, prejudices, and lies perpetuated by society. When Black people are constantly told that they are less than, undeserving, or inferior, it's easy for those messages to take root deep inside. Internalized oppression leads to self-doubt, low self-esteem, and a sense of hopelessness.

In many ways, internalized oppression is like an invisible anchor. It keeps us stuck in a place of emotional paralysis, making it difficult to break free from the patterns of self-destructive thinking and behavior. We might see ourselves as less capable, less valuable, or less deserving of success and happiness. We may doubt our ability to lead, to dream, to be whole.

But this crisis isn't our fault. The responsibility lies with the systems and structures that seek to dehumanize us. The psychological damage is a byproduct of centuries of mistreatment, and it is up to us, both individually and collectively, to begin healing. The fight for our sanity is not just about surviving the trauma, it's about reclaiming our worth, our peace, and our power.

Building a Path Toward Healing

Healing from this crisis starts with acknowledging its existence. We cannot heal what we do not recognize. The first step is to face the truth: this trauma is real, and it is not something we can ignore or wish away. By validating our pain, we can begin to release it. Understanding the depth of this crisis, how it impacts the mind, body, and spirit, helps us frame the conversation in a way that fosters true healing.

Next, we need to talk about mental health. For too long, mental health has been stigmatized in the Black community. There's a long-standing belief that we must endure, that seeking help is a sign of weakness. But in reality, seeking help is an act of strength. It's about showing up for yourself and saying, "I deserve better." It's time to reframe the narrative around mental health in the Black community, acknowledging that we don't have to carry the weight of centuries of trauma alone.

Counseling and therapy are one of the powerful trauma-healing tools but they are not the only solutions. We must also turn to our communities. Collective healing is often more effective than individual efforts. When we come together to support each other, to share our experiences, to understand that our pain is interconnected, we begin to create spaces for healing. In these spaces, we can find the strength to break free from the patterns of internalized oppression and begin to rebuild the emotional infrastructure of our lives.

The Fight for Sanity: A Collective Endeavor

The crisis is real, but so is our power to fight back. We must stand together in this battle for our sanity. We must challenge the systems that perpetuate trauma and destruction. This is not just about personal survival, it's about the survival of an entire community. We must fight to rebuild what has been broken and to create new narratives for ourselves, our children, and the generations to come.

The fight for our sanity begins with the understanding that it is not enough to simply survive. We must strive for thriving, for mental well-being, for emotional and spiritual wholeness. This journey is long, and it will require effort, patience, and resilience. But it is a fight worth undertaking because our sanity, and our future, depends on it.

In the end, healing is not a solitary endeavor. It is a collective one. We are in this together. And together, we can rise. Together, we can heal. Together, we can reclaim our sanity, our peace, and our power. This is the first step in the long journey toward overcoming the psychological crisis that has plagued us for far too long. It's time to start fighting for our sanity, together.

Chapter 2

Epigenetics And The Biological Imprint Of Trauma

CHAPTER 2

Epigenetics And The Biological Imprint Of Trauma

The mind is not the only thing that bears the scars of trauma. For years, we've understood trauma primarily as an emotional or psychological experience, one that we process in our minds, but increasingly, scientific research shows that trauma also leaves a profound imprint on our bodies, influencing us biologically. This chapter will explore how trauma, particularly the generational trauma stemming from slavery and systemic oppression, is biologically encoded in the body through a field of science known as epigenetics.

What is Epigenetics?

Epigenetics is known as the study of gene expression or cellular activity changes that do not involve alterations to the underlying DNA sequence. Various factors can be a cause-roots for these changes including environmental influences, stress, trauma, and even diet. In simpler terms, while your genetic code (DNA) remains the same, epigenetic modifications can turn certain genes "on" or "off," affecting how your body responds to stress and various stimuli. These modifications are not only passed down from one generation to the next but also have long-lasting impacts on a person's mental and physical health.

What makes epigenetics particularly relevant to the discussion of trauma is that it provides a scientific basis for the idea that the pain of the past can be carried forward into future generations. The trauma experienced by one generation, especially severe trauma such as that experienced by enslaved Africans, doesn't just disappear, it can be biologically passed down, influencing the emotional and physical health of descendants.

How Trauma Transforms the Body

The concept of epigenetics sheds new light on how trauma can affect us at a biological level. When a person experiences significant trauma, especially chronic stress or fear, the body releases stress hormones such as cortisol. In the short term, these hormones help the body respond to immediate threats. But cortisol's high levels and its prolonged exposure lead to various negative outcomes, including immune system suppression, cardiovascular problems, and mental health disorders like depression and anxiety.

What's even more alarming is that these effects don't necessarily stay with the person who experienced the trauma. Based on research, traumatic experiences alter the expression of genes relevant to stress response systems, and these changes further pass down to offspring. In essence, the trauma that was experienced by our ancestors during slavery, segregation, and systemic oppression is biologically encoded, affecting the very way we respond to stress and adversity.

Studies in animal models have provided clear evidence of this phenomenon. One groundbreaking study conducted with mice found that those who had experienced traumatic stress showed changes in their epigenetic markers, specifically, modifications to genes that regulate stress response. Even more remarkable, when these mice reproduced, their offspring exhibited similar stress responses, despite never having experienced the original trauma themselves. This is called transgenerational epigenetic inheritance, and it suggests that the outcomes of trauma are biological imprints that affect not only the individual but also their descendants.

The Legacy of Slavery and Its Biological Effects

For Black Americans and descendants of enslaved Africans, this research has profound implications. The trauma of slavery, forced displacement, physical violence, family separation, and systemic degradation, did not end with emancipation. Instead, it has been carried forward through generations, not only in the cultural and social dynamics of Black life but also at a biological level.

Researchers have explored the effects of intergenerational trauma within communities of African descent, particularly focusing on how historical trauma like slavery and colonialism might still be impacting the descendants of those who lived through it. For example, studies have shown that descendants of Holocaust survivors exhibit higher levels of stress-related conditions, and similar trends have been observed in Black communities, where ancestral trauma from slavery, segregation, and ongoing racial discrimination manifests in heightened vulnerability to mental health issues, chronic illnesses, and other stress-related conditions.

This biological transmission of trauma isn't confined to any one group; it's a global phenomenon. But the unique and continuous history of racial oppression faced by African Americans means that the trauma is compounded, becoming part of a cycle that is difficult to break. The very DNA of Black communities holds traces of this historical abuse, and these traces influence how stress is handled, how emotional pain is processed, and even how individuals perceive the world around them.

The Biological Mechanisms: How Trauma Gets Under Skin

One key aspect of epigenetic modifications in response to trauma is the alteration of certain genes that regulate the body's stress response. These include genes related to cortisol production that's a hormone helping the body deal with stress. When trauma is experienced, especially chronic trauma, the body's stress systems become overactivated. This overactivation leads to physical changes in the brain and other organs, contributing to the development of mood disorders, PTSD, and anxiety.

However, the effects are not just neurological. Trauma can also affect how the body metabolizes nutrients, how it fights off infections, and even how it ages. One study found that people who experienced early-life trauma exhibited physical changes in their DNA that could accelerate aging and increase susceptibility to disease. In many ways, trauma makes the body more vulnerable to a range of conditions, from autoimmune diseases to cardiovascular problems.

The Importance of Acknowledging the Biological Impact

While the psychological effects of trauma are often discussed, feelings of anxiety, depression, and emotional numbness, the biological impact is equally important to address. The fact that trauma can alter our very biology is a powerful reminder of the long-term impact of systemic violence and oppression. If trauma can leave a mark on the body, then healing must also take a comprehensive approach, one that includes addressing the biological, psychological, and social dimensions of the trauma.

Recognizing the biological impact of trauma opens up new possibilities for healing. It underscores the need for therapeutic approaches that go beyond traditional talk therapy. Practices such as mindfulness, trauma-informed care, and somatic therapies that address the body's response to trauma can be essential in healing the physical wounds left by generations of abuse. There is also growing evidence that certain lifestyle changes, such as improved nutrition, regular physical activity, and sufficient sleep, can help "reprogram" the body's response to stress and reduce the negative impact of epigenetic changes.

Furthermore, addressing the biological impact of trauma reinforces the need for a collective approach to healing. If trauma has impacted entire communities on a biological level, the path to healing cannot be purely individual. Communities must work together to create environments that promote healing, resilience, and overall well-being. Just as trauma can be passed down from one generation to the next, so too can resilience, healing, and hope.

Rewrite the Epigenetic Story: Reclaim Our Health

The most powerful aspect of epigenetics is its potential for change. Unlike genetic mutations, which are permanent, epigenetic changes can be reversible. This means that through positive lifestyle changes, therapeutic interventions, and social support, it is possible to "rewrite" the biological narrative of trauma. Healing is not just possible, it is within our reach.

By understanding the biological imprint of trauma, we gain more tools to fight back against the systems that continue to perpetuate harm. We can begin to create spaces for healing that not only address the mind but also the body and spirit. Reclaiming our health means reclaiming our future, one where trauma no longer dictates our fate, where we are empowered to rewrite the genetic legacy of our ancestors and build a new future for the generations to come.

This chapter has explored how trauma, particularly the trauma stemming from slavery and racial oppression, can biologically shape our lives. Through the lens of epigenetics, we can see that trauma is not just something we carry in our minds, it's something that lives in our bodies, shaping our responses to the world around us. But we also see the potential for change, for healing, and for rewriting our biological narrative. The path forward involves recognizing the impact of trauma on both our minds and bodies, and taking steps to reclaim our health, our peace, and our power. The fight for healing is a fight that encompasses every aspect of our being, and it is one we must undertake together.

Chapter 3

The Disruption Of Family Structures And Parenting Models

CHAPTER 3

The Disruption Of Family Structures And Parenting Models

The family has always been the cornerstone of society, providing individuals with the emotional, social, and financial support necessary for survival and growth. However, the trauma inflicted by slavery, systemic oppression, and racial discrimination has disrupted the foundational structures of family life for Black communities, leaving deep, lasting effects. This chapter explores how these historical and social forces have altered family dynamics and parenting models within Black families, often leading to cycles of disruption, instability, and generational trauma.

The Impact of Slavery on Family Structure

The institution of slavery was built upon the systematic destruction of family ties among Black people. Enslaved Africans were often forcibly separated from their families upon arrival in the Americas. Families including parents, husbands-wives, and children were sold to different plantations, ripped from one another without any regard for familial bonds. This brutality not only shattered the basic unit of the family but also created lasting emotional scars.

Enslaved individuals had no control over their family structure, no ability to protect their loved ones from the violence and oppression that surrounded them. In many cases, enslaved mothers had to watch their children be taken away or sold, knowing they had little to no power to protect them. Fathers were similarly powerless, unable to provide the emotional or financial support expected of them in a traditional family role. This constant separation and emotional distress created a long-lasting disruption in the way Black families functioned.

While slavery ended over 150 years ago, its effects on family structures continue to echo through Black communities. The loss of stable family structures due to slavery laid the groundwork for later challenges in parenting and family dynamics. The resulting emotional trauma, insecurity, and lack of family unity contributed to ongoing struggles within Black families, where generations often struggled to maintain and nurture strong family bonds.

The Legacy of Family Disruption: Generational Effects

The trauma experienced by enslaved ancestors didn't disappear with the abolition of slavery. It was passed down to future generations, creating a cycle of instability within family structures. The absence of strong, supportive family units during the period of slavery left lasting consequences, including an inability to model healthy, stable relationships for children. The idea of family cohesion and the role of parents in nurturing children became skewed by centuries of trauma and dislocation.

The disruption of Black family structures was further exacerbated by Jim Crow laws, segregation, and economic disenfranchisement. As Black families continued to face systemic oppression, many were forced to live in poverty and were subjected to violence and discrimination. Economic instability often led to a lack of resources for proper child-rearing, leading to further disruption in family life. With the constant threat of economic and social marginalization, many parents struggled to provide for their children, both emotionally and financially.

These challenges were compounded by a deep mistrust of institutions, including the education system and social services. The historical experiences of Black people with these institutions, ranging from enslavement to state-sponsored violence, fostered a skepticism that was passed down to children. The inability to rely on societal systems for support often meant that Black families had to be self-reliant, even at the cost of emotional well-being and stability.

Parenting in a Systemic Context: Raising Children Under Duress

Parenting in the face of systemic oppression and ongoing trauma is not only challenging but also often misunderstood. Black parents have had to raise their children in environments that constantly threaten their safety, dignity, and sense of belonging. From a young age, Black children are forced to navigate a world that marginalizes them based on their race, and this external pressure often affects the way they are parented.

One of the primary issues faced by Black parents is the need to prepare their children for the harsh realities of racism and discrimination. This "racial socialization" involves equipping children with the tools they need to survive and thrive in a world that is often hostile to them. While this is a protective measure, it can also be an emotionally taxing responsibility for parents, who may feel the weight of constantly preparing their children for societal challenges, often at the expense of fostering a carefree childhood.

In many Black families, especially those with histories of trauma, parenting styles have been shaped by survival. Generations of parents have been forced to be overly protective or overly strict, sometimes in an attempt to shield their children from the dangers of racism, poverty, or violence. These parenting approaches, rooted in a survival mentality, can lead to difficulties in nurturing emotionally healthy relationships. While the intent is to protect, the unintended consequence is often an emotional distance that makes it hard for children to feel secure, loved, or understood.

Moreover, many Black parents, particularly those in underprivileged areas, face additional challenges, such as poverty, inadequate education, and unstable housing. These stressors can lead to frustration, burnout, and difficulty maintaining a healthy balance between work, home life, and self-care. Parenting in such circumstances often means navigating trauma while simultaneously trying to be emotionally available and supportive. This complex dynamic can lead to generational patterns of emotional repression, where children grow up learning to suppress their feelings, fears, and anxieties in order to avoid burdening their parents.

The Disruption of the Family Through Incarceration

Another critical factor in the disruption of Black family structures is the over-incarceration of Black men. The prison industrial complex has disproportionately targeted Black communities that leads to high rates of incarceration among Black men. As a result, many Black families are torn apart by the absence of fathers and male role models. This absence has significant emotional and psychological effects on children, particularly boys, who may lack male guidance and support.

The effects of having a parent incarcerated can be long-lasting. Children with incarcerated parents often experience instability, poor academic performance, and emotional distress. The absence of a father figure can lead to a breakdown in the familial support system, leaving children to cope with the strain of growing up without a key emotional anchor. Mothers are often left to shoulder the burdens of raising children alone, which further exacerbates the stress and emotional strain on the family unit.

The intersection of race and mass incarceration creates a vicious cycle, where Black families are continuously destabilized by the systemic over-policing and criminalization of Black bodies. The trauma inflicted by the separation of families due to incarceration has been another form of family disruption that compounds the struggles of Black communities.

Healing and Rebuilding Family Structures

While the trauma caused by the disruption of family structures is deeply ingrained, there is hope. Healing begins with acknowledging the impact of systemic oppression on Black families and recognizing the need for restoration. Rebuilding family structures requires addressing the root causes of family instability and creating environments that promote emotional health, resilience, and connection.

One way to begin healing is by redefining what family means. Family does not have to be defined by traditional structures alone. Extended family, close-knit community networks, and mentorship can provide the emotional support and stability that children and parents need to thrive. By investing in community-based resources, Black families can get the required support they need to navigate the challenges they face.

Furthermore, therapy and mental health care are crucial tools for healing generational trauma within families. Therapy treatment provides a safe space for children and parents to express their emotions, understand their trauma, and develop healthier coping strategies. Rebuilding trust within families requires emotional openness, vulnerability, and patience, qualities that can be cultivated through intentional therapy and community support.

Finally, it is essential to reclaim the power of parenting. Black parents can work together to develop healthier models of parenting, models that emphasize emotional availability, understanding, and nurturing, rather than simply focusing on survival. Empowering Black families with the tools and knowledge they need to break cycles of trauma will help create stronger, more stable family units that can withstand the pressures of systemic oppression.

Reclaim Family and Parenting Models

The disruption of family structures and parenting models within Black communities is a direct result of historical trauma, systemic racism, and socio-economic disenfranchisement. However, while these forces have worked to tear families apart, there is immense power in reclaiming and rebuilding the family unit. Through therapy, community support, and redefining family roles, Black families can heal from the wounds of the past and create stronger, more resilient bonds for future generations. Healing from family disruption requires acknowledging the pain of the past, while working toward a future where Black families can thrive and support one another in the face of adversity.

Chapter 4

The Economics of Trauma

CHAPTER 4

The Economics of Trauma

Generational Wealth and Financial PTSD

The lingering effects of trauma are not only emotional and psychological; they are also economic. In Black communities, the history of slavery, segregation, and systemic racism has shaped not just cultural and personal identities but also economic realities. The trauma of centuries of economic disenfranchisement and exclusion continues to reverberate in the financial lives of Black individuals and families. This chapter explores the intersection of trauma and economics, with a focus on generational wealth, financial PTSD, and the lasting impact of economic oppression.

The Origins of Economic Trauma

The roots of economic trauma in Black communities are deeply entwined with the history of slavery and its aftermath. During slavery, Black people were systematically stripped of their rights to accumulate wealth, own property, or pass on assets to future generations. Enslaved individuals were treated as property themselves, and any wealth they generated went directly into the pockets of slave owners. As a result, Black families were denied the opportunity to build generational wealth, an opportunity that was readily available to white families, who had access to land, property, and the means to accumulate wealth across generations.

Even after emancipation, Black people were subjected to policies and practices that continued to limit their economic mobility. Laws like Jim Crow and Black Codes segregation restricted access to education, employment, and property ownership. The so-called "sharecropping" system, which replaced slavery in the South, was little more than a modern form of economic exploitation. Even as Black families labored, they were never able to accumulate wealth at the same rate as their white counterparts, creating a permanent economic underclass.

Despite the Civil Rights Movement progress and the efforts of Black entrepreneurs, the legacy of economic oppression remains. Generations of Black families have been denied the ability to build and pass on wealth, resulting in Black-white households' wealth gap. According to reports, the median net worth of Black families is a fraction of that of white families, with the gap continuing to widen over time.

Generational Wealth: A Legacy of Disinvestment

One of the most significant consequences of this history is the inability of many Black families to build generational wealth. Wealth is typically passed down from one generation to the next, providing opportunities for children to access education, own property, start businesses, and achieve financial independence. However, because Black families were systematically excluded from wealth-building opportunities for so long, many are still struggling to accumulate assets.

Without wealth, Black families are more likely to experience financial insecurity, living paycheck to paycheck without a safety net in place. This lack of financial security creates a vicious cycle of poverty, where each generation must work harder to survive without the cushion of inherited wealth or intergenerational financial support. The absence of generational wealth also limits access to opportunities such as homeownership, higher education, and business ownership, key factors that can lead to long-term financial stability and upward mobility.

The challenge of accumulating wealth is compounded by the reality of living in a society where Black individuals are often denied equal access to economic opportunities. Discriminatory practices such as redlining, racial profiling in lending, and discriminatory hiring practices continue to prevent Black families from building wealth at the same rate as their white counterparts. Even today, Black entrepreneurs often face higher barriers to securing funding for their businesses, and mortgages or subprime loans are more likely to be denied for Black homebuyers. As a result, the cycle of economic exclusion continues, leaving many Black families without the resources needed to break free from financial instability.

Financial PTSD: The Emotional Impact of Economic Trauma

The trauma of economic disenfranchisement extends beyond the tangible effects of poverty and wealth inequality. Financial hardship and the inability to build wealth can create a unique form of psychological distress known as financial PTSD. Just as individuals who experience violent trauma or abuse may develop post-traumatic stress disorder (PTSD), those who experience ongoing financial instability and deprivation can develop a form of PTSD that manifests in chronic anxiety, fear of financial insecurity, and an overwhelming sense of hopelessness.

For many Black individuals, financial PTSD manifests in a pervasive sense of financial anxiety, where even small setbacks, such as an unexpected medical bill or a car repair, can trigger feelings of panic and helplessness. This anxiety is rooted in the fear of losing what little stability has been gained and the knowledge that, for many, there is no safety net to fall back on. The emotional toll of constantly living in financial stress can affect overall well-being including relationships and mental health.

Financial PTSD also contributes to unhealthy financial behaviors, such as hoarding, overwork, or a reluctance to seek help when needed. Many Black individuals, especially those from economically disadvantaged backgrounds, are taught to "make do" and "pull themselves up by their bootstraps." This mindset, while rooted in resilience, can also prevent individuals from addressing the deeper emotional wounds of financial trauma. It can create a sense of shame around financial struggles, which in turn leads to avoidance of seeking assistance or engaging in financial planning.

The Cycle of Poverty: The Cost of Financial Trauma

The cost of financial trauma is not just psychological, it's physical, social, and economic. Financial instability stress contributes to several health problems, including heart disease, hypertension, and mental health disorders. The continued worry about making ends meet or losing financial stability can lead to chronic stress, which has been shown to negatively affect both mental and physical health.

Additionally, insufficient financial resources makes it harder for Black families to access quality healthcare, education, and housing. These disparities create a compounding effect, where financial hardship leads to poor health outcomes, which in turn makes it even harder to break free from poverty. This cycle perpetuates itself, as families who experience financial hardship are less likely to accumulate savings, invest in education, or access opportunities that could improve their economic status.

The inability to build wealth also limits the ability to pass on resources to the next generation, ensuring that future generations will continue to struggle with the same economic challenges. This is why the wealth gap between Black and white families is so persistent and difficult to close, each generation is burdened by the weight of the previous generation's economic trauma.

Break the Cycle: Healing Financial Trauma

Despite the deep-rooted nature of financial trauma, ways are available to break the cycle and begin healing. Addressing the economics of trauma requires both systemic change and individual financial empowerment. On a larger scale, policies that promote equitable access to education, healthcare, housing, and business opportunities are essential for closing the racial wealth gap. These policies should include measures such as targeted investment in Black communities, the elimination of discriminatory practices in lending and hiring, and greater access to wealth-building tools like homeownership and small business loans.

On an individual level, healing from financial trauma requires a combination of financial education, emotional support, and mental health care. Financial literacy is a key tool for empowering individuals to make informed decisions about their money, budgeting, saving, and investing. Effective financial management can break free individuals from the cycle of financial instability and work toward building wealth.

The emotional and psychological effects of financial trauma are equally important. Financial PTSD is real, and it can be debilitating. Mental health care like therapy and support groups, can help individuals address the emotional wounds of economic oppression. By acknowledging and processing the psychological effects of financial trauma, individuals can start healing and develop healthier relationships with money.

Finally, community-based solutions are crucial for breaking the cycle of economic trauma. By coming together to share resources, support one another, and advocate for systemic change, Black communities can create networks of economic support that help individuals thrive. These community-based networks can provide mentorship, financial counseling, and collective action that empowers individuals and families to build wealth and overcome financial hardship.

The Path Forward

The economics of trauma are complex, but they are not insurmountable. By understanding the ways in which generational wealth and financial PTSD have shaped the economic realities of Black communities, we can begin to heal the wounds of economic oppression. It will take a combination of systemic change, financial education, emotional healing, and community support to break the cycle of economic trauma and create a future where Black families can build and pass on wealth.

The road to financial healing is not easy, but it is possible. By confronting the economic legacy of trauma and working together to address the inequities that have long held Black communities back, we can begin to rebuild a more equitable and just economic future. The fight for economic justice is an essential part of the broader racial equality struggle, and it begins with acknowledging the deep, lasting impact of financial trauma and taking the necessary steps to heal and rebuild.

Chapter 5

Internalized Oppression And Cultural Identity Crisis

CHAPTER 5

Internalized Oppression And Cultural Identity Crisis

Internalized oppression refers to the process by which individuals from marginalized groups adopt and internalize the negative beliefs, stereotypes, and biases about themselves and their community that are perpetuated by dominant societies. For Black people, internalized oppression is a pervasive and complex challenge that manifests in a wide range of emotional, social, and psychological difficulties. This chapter explores how the historical and ongoing experience of racism, segregation, and systemic oppression has led to a crisis of cultural identity, where Black individuals and communities often struggle with feelings of inferiority, shame, and disconnection from their cultural roots.

The Birth of Internalized Oppression

The origins of internalized oppression can be traced back to the period of slavery, when the dehumanization of Black people was not only institutionalized but also deeply embedded in the psychological fabric of society. During slavery, Black people were taught to see themselves as inferior to white people. The idea of Black inferiority was propagated through various means, whether through legal systems, religious doctrines, or the pseudoscience of the time. Black people were forced to believe that they were less intelligent, less capable, and less deserving of respect and dignity than their white counterparts.

The violence and brutality of slavery were designed not just to control Black bodies but to erode the sense of self-worth and identity among enslaved people. The forced separation of families, the stripping of names, and the continuous exposure to brutality had devastating effects on the psyche of Black people. Enslaved individuals were denied their humanity, their culture, and their sense of belonging. The psychological damage from this brutal dehumanization did not end with the abolition of slavery, it persisted through the Civil Rights Movement, the Jim Crow segregation, and continues to affect Black people today in the form of systemic racism and microaggressions.

Internalized oppression can manifest in many ways. It might show up in how individuals view themselves, how they relate to their community, and how they interact with the larger society. Some common symptoms of internalized oppression include feelings of shame, self-hatred, and a lack of pride in one's heritage or identity. These feelings can be reinforced by negative portrayals of Black people in the media, in politics, and in popular culture, which often perpetuate harmful stereotypes and portray Blackness as something to be ashamed of or avoided.

The Psychological Toll of Internalized Oppression

The psychological impact of internalized oppression can be profound and far-reaching. The constant bombardment of negative images and stereotypes can create a sense of inferiority, causing Black individuals to doubt their worth and question their potential. This internalized belief in one's inadequacy can lead to feelings of anxiety, depression, and a deep sense of helplessness.

One of the most damaging effects of internalized oppression is that it can erode a person's sense of self-love and self-respect. Black individuals who internalize negative stereotypes may begin to see themselves through the lens of those stereotypes, whether it's seeing themselves as less intelligent, less capable, or less deserving of success. This diminished self-esteem can lead to avoidance of opportunities for growth and achievement, as individuals may feel unworthy or unqualified to pursue their goals.

In addition to these individual effects, internalized oppression can also have a profound impact on Black relationships. Individuals who struggle with internalized oppression may have difficulty forming healthy, supportive relationships with others in their community. Feelings of inadequacy or self-hatred can lead to social isolation, mistrust, and difficulty in forming intimate bonds with others. This isolation is further compounded by a lack of role models or positive representations of Black people in positions of power, success, and influence.

The trauma of internalized oppression can also affect how Black people raise their children. When parents internalize feelings of inferiority or shame, they may unconsciously pass these beliefs on to the next generation. This cycle of internalized oppression can perpetuate itself, leading to a deepening crisis of cultural identity in subsequent generations.

Cultural Identity Crisis: The Struggle for Belonging

A significant component of internalized oppression is the cultural identity crisis that many Black people face. For centuries, Black people in America (and other parts of the world) have been told that their culture is inferior, primitive, and something to be discarded or "civilized." From the forced removal of African cultural practices during slavery to the continued erasure of Black history and contributions in mainstream society, Black culture has been denigrated and marginalized.

This erasure of cultural heritage creates a crisis of identity for Black people, many of whom struggle to reconcile their heritage with the dominant culture's negative portrayals of their identity. As a result, some individuals may feel disconnected from their African roots, unsure of where they fit within their own culture or within broader society. They may seek to adopt cultural norms and practices that are alien to their heritage, in an effort to "fit in" or be accepted by mainstream society.

This crisis of cultural identity is especially evident among Black youth, who are often exposed to conflicting messages about their identity. On one hand, they may be taught to embrace Black culture and history; on the other, they are bombarded with negative stereotypes that paint Blackness as something undesirable. This tension can lead to confusion and a sense of disconnection as young people struggle to understand who they are and where they belong.

For many Black individuals, the process of reclaiming their cultural identity is a difficult but necessary journey. It involves confronting the negative messages about Blackness that have been internalized over time and re-connecting with the rich history, traditions, and achievements of African and African American culture. This process of self-discovery and self-acceptance is crucial for overcoming internalized oppression and for cultivating a sense of pride and self-worth.

Break the Chains: Reclaim Cultural Identity

Reclaiming one's cultural identity is an essential step in healing from internalized oppression. It requires individuals to actively challenge the negative messages they have internalized and to cultivate a positive and affirming relationship with their heritage. This process involves learning about the history, contributions, and achievements of Black people throughout the world, and embracing the diverse cultural traditions that make Black identity unique and powerful.

One of the key steps in overcoming internalized oppression is deconstructing the harmful stereotypes that have been perpetuated for centuries. Black people must begin to recognize the ways in which they have been misrepresented and mischaracterized, and work to redefine what it means to be Black. This means celebrating Blackness in all its forms, whether through art, music, literature, or history, and rejecting the limiting and dehumanizing portrayals of Black people that have been ingrained in society.

Healing from internalized oppression also involves developing a strong sense of community and solidarity with other Black people. This sense of connection can provide the emotional support and validation that individuals need to combat feelings of isolation and shame. By working together, Black individuals can create spaces where their identities are affirmed and celebrated and where they can support one another in the healing process.

Finally, mental health support is crucial in overcoming the psychological toll of internalized oppression. Therapy and counseling, and also support groups provide individuals with the tools they need to process the trauma of internalized racism and develop healthier self-concepts. Healing from internalized oppression is not an overnight process, it requires time, self-compassion, and a willingness to confront the deep-rooted beliefs that have shaped one's sense of self.

Reclaim Power and Identity

Internalized oppression and the cultural identity crisis are significant barriers to the emotional and psychological well-being of Black people. However, by acknowledging the impact of systemic racism and actively working to reclaim their cultural heritage, Black individuals can begin to heal from the wounds of internalized oppression. This process requires self-awareness, community support, and a commitment to redefining Black identity on their own terms.

The journey of healing from internalized oppression is transformative, it is a journey of reclaiming power, pride, and a sense of belonging. Through self-acceptance, cultural reclamation, and collective solidarity, Black people can overcome the psychological impact of internalized oppression and build a future where their identities are no longer defined by the trauma of the past but by the strength, resilience, and beauty of their heritage.

Chapter 6

What If Death Seems Like The Best End To Pain

CHAPTER 6

What If Death Seems Like the Best End To Pain

Suicidal thoughts and despair feelings are the result of prolonged suffering, trauma, and hopelessness. For many who experience deep psychological pain, especially those dealing with the effects of Post-Traumatic Slave Syndrome (PTSS), suicide may seem like the only way to escape unbearable emotional distress. But there is another path. If you are struggling with these thoughts, know this: you are not alone, and your pain is not the end of your story.

This chapter is dedicated to those who feel like they are drowning in their pain, to those who have contemplated ending their lives, and to those who need a reason to hold on. It is a message of hope and survival, offering real steps toward relief, healing, and a life worth living.

Understanding the Depth of the Pain

Feeling like death is the only way out is often the result of long-term emotional suffering. That suffering may come from different places:

- *Generational Trauma:* The pain of oppression, racism, poverty, and violence can accumulate over generations, leading to feelings of helplessness and despair.
- *Personal Trauma:* Abuse, neglect, family dysfunction, and personal losses can leave deep wounds that are difficult to heal.
- *Mental Health Struggles:* Depression, anxiety, PTSD, and other mental health conditions create difficulty to see hope beyond the pain.
- *Societal Pressures and Systemic Racism:* Feeling unseen, unheard, and undervalued in a world that often dismisses Black pain can intensify feelings of isolation.

Suicidal thoughts don't mean you are weak or broken. They are signals that you have been carrying too much pain for too long. If no one has told you this yet, your pain is real, but it is not your fault.

What to Do Right Now If You Feel Like Giving Up

When you are in the depths of suicidal thoughts, everything can feel overwhelming. You may not see a way forward. But at this moment, the goal is not to solve everything, it's to get through this moment.

1. Breathe. Slow Down. Focus on the Next Five Minutes.

When pain feels unbearable, surviving the next five minutes is a victory. Focus only on what is immediately in front of you. Try this:

- Breathe-in for 4 seconds then hold for 4 seconds, and exhale for 4 seconds. Repeat.
- Touch something around you, a chair, a blanket, your own skin. Remind yourself you are here, alive, right now.
- Say something kind to yourself: "I'm still here. I'm fighting. I will give myself more time."

2. Say It Out Loud: "I Need Help."

One of the most powerful things you can do at this moment is reach out. Tell someone what you are feeling.

- Call a trusted friend or family member. You don't have to explain everything, just say, "I'm struggling, and I need help."
- If you don't feel comfortable talking to someone you know, reach out to a mental health professional or crisis hotline. There are people whose job is to support you at this moment.

3. Remove Immediate Means of Harm

If you are having strong urges to hurt yourself, remove anything in your environment that could be dangerous. Give yourself space and time to work through this moment.

- If you have access to anything that could cause harm, put it away or leave the room.
- Call someone and let them know you are struggling so they can help you stay safe.

- If necessary, go somewhere you feel safer, whether it's a friend's house, a public space, or a mental health facility.

4. Remind Yourself: This Feeling Will Pass

Suicidal thoughts are temporary, even though they feel permanent. You have survived every painful moment in your past, this one will not break you either.

Try to recall a moment when you were in pain but found relief. What helped you back then? Can you do that now?

Break the Cycle of Despair

While immediate survival is the priority, true healing requires long-term action. Here are key steps to help shift from crisis mode to rebuilding a life worth living:

1. Find a Support System

No one heals in isolation. Finding the right support can make all the difference:

- Therapists and counselors trained in racial trauma and mental health can provide professional guidance.
- Community groups and support circles (online or in person) offer safe spaces to share and heal with others who understand.
- Spiritual or faith-based communities can provide a sense of belonging and hope.
- Trusted friends or mentors can remind you that you are loved, valued, and needed.

2. Address the Root of the Pain

Instead of just pushing through the pain, work to understand where it comes from:

- Is it linked to past trauma?
- Is it connected to feelings of worthlessness or failure?
- Are you carrying emotional wounds from racism, family struggles, or society?

Healing starts when you acknowledge the pain and allow yourself to seek relief.

3. Reconnect With Yourself

When depression and suicidal thoughts take over, they can make you feel like you are nothing more than your pain. But you are more.

Try these small but powerful ways to reconnect with yourself:

- Write a letter to your future self about what you are feeling right now and why you are choosing to keep going.
- Engage in something creative, music, art, journaling, movement, anything that helps express what words cannot.
- Move your body, even if it's just stepping outside for a few minutes. Physical movement can help shift mental energy.
- Create a "Reasons to Live" List, even if it only has one thing on it right now.

4. Challenge the Lies Depression Tells You

Suicidal thoughts often come with lies:

- "I am a burden." (You are not, you are loved.)
- "No one will miss me." (Someone will. Many will.)
- "I will never feel better." (You will. Healing is possible.)

Whenever these thoughts come up, challenge them. Replace them with small affirmations of hope:

- "I am in pain, but I am not worthless."
- "I am struggling, but I am still here."
- "I may not see the way forward yet, but I will give myself time to find it."

Reaching for Life, Even in the Darkness

Choosing to live does not mean the pain disappears overnight. It means believing that another version of your life is possible, one with joy, love, and healing.

Right now, you may not believe that better days are coming. That's okay. For now, just focus on staying. Stay for the next sunrise. Stay for the next song that makes you feel something. Stay for the small joys you haven't yet discovered.

Your life is valuable. Your pain is real, but so is your capacity to heal. You are not alone, and you are not beyond help.

If no one has told you today, I want you to stay.

Chapter 7

Poor Diet, Neglected Health, Addiction, And Low-Key Suicide

CHAPTER 7

Poor Diet, Neglected Health, Addiction, And Low-Key Suicide

The slowest form of suicide isn't always an intentional act, it's the gradual destruction of the body and mind through neglect, addiction, and poor lifestyle choices. Many people don't realize that their daily habits are slowly taking their lives away. Poor diet, substance abuse, untreated health issues, and self-destructive behaviors are all ways in which deep-seated pain manifests.

For many Black individuals dealing with Post-Traumatic Slave Syndrome (PTSS), the physical, emotional, and psychological toll of generational trauma leads to unhealthy coping mechanisms. What looks like mere bad habits, overeating, drug or alcohol use, ignoring medical problems, can often be an unconscious form of self-harm. This chapter explores how these slow and subtle forms of self-destruction operate and, more importantly, how to break free from them.

The Link Between Trauma and Self-Destruction

When people go through trauma, their nervous system shifts into survival mode. This survival state can lead to high levels of stress, anxiety, and emotional numbness. Over time, many turn to self-destructive behaviors to numb pain, cope with stress, or regain a sense of control.

Some of these behaviors include:

- Eating unhealthy foods for comfort, even when they lead to obesity, diabetes, and heart disease.
- Abusing alcohol, drugs, or cigarettes to escape emotional pain.
- Ignoring chronic illnesses and refusing medical care, even when symptoms worsen.
- Engaging in reckless behavior, like dangerous sex, excessive gambling, or financial self-sabotage.

The sad reality is that for many Black individuals, poor health choices aren't just about individual behavior. They are deeply tied to historical oppression, food deserts, medical discrimination, and systemic inequalities. To take your first step towards breaking free, you need to understand these connections well.

Poor Diet: The Silent Killer

Food is supposed to nourish, heal, and sustain us. But for many in Black communities, food has become a slow weapon of self-destruction.

1. The History of Unhealthy Eating Habits

Many of the eating habits that exist today in Black communities were shaped by historical circumstances. During slavery and segregation, Black people had limited access to quality food and were forced to survive on scraps. This led to the creation of high-fat, high-salt, high-sugar meals that, while delicious, were often unhealthy. Over time, these eating habits became cultural norms, passed down through generations.

Fast forward to today, and many Black communities still suffer from food deserts, areas where fresh, healthy food is hard to find. Fast food and processed meals become the default, leading to higher rates of obesity, diabetes, hypertension, and heart disease.

2. Emotional Eating: When Food Becomes a Drug

For many, food is more than just sustenance, it's a coping mechanism. Stress, depression, and anxiety often trigger overeating, particularly of high-calorie, sugary, or fatty foods. This is because eating releases dopamine, the brain's "feel-good" chemical.

However, the short-term relief of emotional eating leads to long-term damage. Obesity, high blood pressure, and diabetes don't just happen overnight, they develop over years of self-neglect.

3. Break the Cycle: Heal Through Nutrition

- Reclaim food as medicine: Shift from eating for comfort to eating for healing.
- Make small changes: Swap out sugary drinks for water, add more vegetables to meals, and cook at home instead of eating processed food.
- Challenge cultural food myths: Not all "soul food" has to be unhealthy. Traditional African diets were plant-based and nutrient-rich. Reconnect with these roots.

Addiction: Escaping Pain, Finding More Pain

Substance abuse, whether alcohol, drugs, or even prescription medication, often starts as a way to cope. People drink or use drugs to forget their struggles, but addiction only deepens the pain.

1. The Role of Trauma in Addiction

Generational trauma creates high levels of stress hormones in the body. Over time, the brain seeks relief through dopamine-boosting substances like alcohol, nicotine, and opioids. This is why addiction is common among individuals who have faced long-term stress and oppression.

2. Alcohol: The Socially Acceptable Poison

Alcoholism is often dismissed because drinking is socially accepted.

However, excessive drinking leads to:

- Liver disease
- Increased depression and anxiety
- Poor decision-making and violent behavior
- Higher suicide risk

Many people drink not to enjoy themselves but to numb their pain. Recognizing the difference is crucial.

3. Drugs: Self-Medication with Deadly Consequences

From weed to cocaine to opioids, many Black individuals turn to drugs to deal with stress, trauma, and pain. However, drug addiction disproportionately affects Black communities due to harsher policing, fewer rehab resources, and the criminalization of substance abuse.

To break the cycle, addiction needs to be seen as a mental health issue, not a moral failure. Seeking help is not weakness, it's a step toward reclaiming life.

Neglected Health: The Price of Avoidance

Many Black people avoid doctors, not out of laziness, but out of deep distrust in the medical system, a distrust that is justified. From the Tuskegee Experiment to the high Black maternal mortality rate, history has shown that Black bodies are often treated with disregard.

However, ignoring health issues only gives them more power. Chronic illnesses like hypertension, diabetes, and cancer don't go away by themselves. The longer they are ignored, the harder they are to treat.

1. Why Black People Avoid the Doctor

- Medical racism: Many Black patients feel unheard or mistreated by healthcare professionals.
- Financial barriers: Lack of insurance and expensive healthcare prevent people from seeking treatment.
- Fear of bad news: Some avoid the doctor because they don't want to hear a diagnosis they can't afford to treat.

2. How to Prioritize Health Without Fear

- Find Black-friendly doctors: Look for healthcare providers who understand Black health concerns.
- Take small steps: Annual checkups, regular exercise, and simple dietary changes can prevent major diseases.
- Advocate for yourself: If a doctor dismisses your symptoms, seek a second opinion. Your health matters.

Low-Key Suicide: When Living Becomes Slow Dying

Not all suicide is immediate. Some people engage in passive self-destruction, where they knowingly or unknowingly engage in behaviors that shorten their lifespan.

Signs of low-key suicide include:

- Refusing medical care for treatable illnesses
- Excessive drinking and drug use despite knowing the risks

- Reckless behaviors (speeding, unprotected sex, financial self-sabotage)
- Chronic stress and overworking without rest or self-care

These behaviors are often unconscious cries for help. The person may not actively want to die but may feel unworthy of living well.

Break the Pattern: Choosing Life, Even in Pain

- Acknowledge self-destructive habits: Awareness is the first step to change.
- Replace harmful coping mechanisms with healthier alternatives like therapy, journaling, or meditation.
- Seek support: Community, mental health professionals, and loved ones can help pull you out of self-destruction.
- Set small health goals: Instead of drastic changes, aim for gradual improvements in diet, exercise, and self-care.

Choosing to Live: The First Step Toward Healing

Poor diet, addiction, and neglected health are not just personal choices, they are symptoms of deeper wounds. Healing requires addressing both the behaviors and the trauma behind them.

If you see yourself in any of these patterns, know this: It's not too late to change. Your life is valuable, and your health is worth fighting for. Even small changes contribute to a healthier and more fulfilling future.

You deserve more than just survival. You deserve to live.

Chapter 8

The Anxiety And Depression Beneath It All

CHAPTER 8

The Anxiety And Depression Beneath It All

Anxiety and depression are silent killers, creeping into the lives of millions, often unnoticed, often untreated. For Black individuals dealing with Post-Traumatic Slave Syndrome (PTSS), these mental health struggles are not just personal burdens but deeply rooted in generational trauma, systemic oppression, and societal neglect.

Anxiety and depression don't always look like what we see in medical textbooks. Sometimes, they manifest as constant exhaustion, irritability, overworking, or shutting down emotionally. Many people don't even realize they're suffering because they've been conditioned to believe that their struggles are just a part of life.

But they are more than that. They are real, they are heavy, and they are treatable. This chapter explores the deep connection between PTSS, anxiety, and depression, and how to begin reclaiming mental health in a world that often tries to break it.

The Weight of Unseen Pain

Black individuals carry more than just their personal struggles; they carry the weight of historical trauma, racial stress, and intergenerational grief. Anxiety and depression are not just individual afflictions, they are deeply linked to external forces that have shaped Black existence for centuries.

1. The Anxiety of Black Survival

Anxiety is more than just nervousness, it's the body's response to real or perceived threats. For Black people, those threats are everywhere:

- The fear of being discriminated against at work, in school, or in public.
- The anxiety of interactions with law enforcement.
- The financial stress of systemic economic barriers.
- The burden of always having to prove one's worth in a society that devalues Black life.

Many Black individuals exist in a constant state of hypervigilance, always scanning for danger. Over time, this chronic stress takes a toll on the body and mind. It leads to:

- Insomnia or restless sleep.
- Chronic fatigue, even after resting.
- A racing heart or panic attacks.
- Digestive issues, headaches, and muscle tension.

This isn't just "stress." It's trauma manifesting in the body.

2. The Depression No One Talks About

Depression in Black communities is often overlooked or misdiagnosed. Instead of being seen as a medical condition, it's dismissed as laziness, moodiness, or weakness. Many Black individuals suffer in silence because:

- They were taught to "push through" rather than seek help.
- They don't want to be seen as weak.
- They fear being judged, even by their own community.
- They lack access to mental health resources.

Depression in Black people doesn't always look like sadness. It can look like:

- Irritability and anger.
- Emotional numbness, feeling disconnected from life.
- Overworking and perfectionism, to escape feelings of inadequacy.
- Physical symptoms like headaches, chronic pain, or digestive problems.

It's easy to think, "I'm just tired," or "I just need to work harder." But ignoring depression doesn't make it go away. It makes it worse.

How Trauma Fuels Anxiety and Depression

Post-Traumatic Slave Syndrome (PTSS) plays a significant role in Black mental health. Generational trauma is passed down not just through culture and family behavior, but also through epigenetics, biological changes that make descendants of the enslaved more vulnerable to stress.

Black people often grow up with trauma responses that feel normal:

- Over-apologizing or shrinking in public spaces (fear of confrontation).
- Overachieving or people-pleasing (to prove worthiness).
- Fear of resting or slowing down (because survival has always required constant movement).
- Emotionally shutting down (because feeling too much hurts).

These are survival tactics, not personality traits. They are the mind's way of coping with a world that has never felt safe.

Break the Stigma: Mental Health Is Not Weakness

Stigma is one of the biggest barriers to healing surrounding mental health in Black communities. There's a long history of viewing therapy as something "white people do" or something that makes a person look crazy.

But therapy isn't a weakness. Asking for help isn't failure. It's survival.

1. Therapy as a Tool for Rebuilding

Finding a Black therapist, or a therapist who understands racial trauma, can be a game-changer. Therapy enables:

- A safe space to express judgment-free emotions.

- Tools to manage anxiety and depression.
- A way to break generational cycles of trauma.

For those who fear therapy, start small:

- Follow Black mental health advocates online.
- Listen to podcasts or read books about Black mental wellness.
- Join support groups that discuss mental health openly.

2. The Role of Spirituality and Community

For many Black people, faith and spirituality play a vital role in mental health. But prayer alone is not always enough. Healing requires a combination of faith, therapy, self-care, and community support.

Some powerful healing tools include:

- Journaling to release bottled-up emotions.
- Meditation and mindfulness to quiet the racing mind.
- Community healing spaces where Black people can discuss their pain openly.
- Culturally relevant self-care, music, art, movement, and storytelling.

Practical Steps to Manage Anxiety and Depression

Mental health struggles don't disappear overnight, but small steps can lead to big changes.

1. Check In With Yourself Daily

Ask:

- "What am I feeling right now?"
- "What do I need today, rest, movement, connection?"
- "What small thing can I do for myself right now?"

2. Move Your Body

Exercise isn't just about fitness, it's about releasing stress. Even small movements, like stretching or walking, help regulate the nervous system.

3. Improve Sleep Habits

Sleep is essential for mental health.

- Avoid screens before bed.
- Develop a nighttime routine.
- Try deep breathing or calming music before sleep.

4. Nourish Your Body and Mind

- Eat foods that fuel the brain, greens, nuts, lean proteins.
- Hydrate. Dehydration increases anxiety and fatigue.
- Limit alcohol and caffeine, they intensify anxiety and depression.

5. Build a Support System

Surround yourself with people who uplift you. Cut off toxic relationships that drain you. You deserve to be around people who care.

6. Set Boundaries

You don't have to be available to everyone all the time.
Protect your peace. Learn to say NO without guilt.

7. Give Yourself Grace

You are not broken. You are healing. Progress is not always linear, some days will be hard. That's okay. Keep going.

You Are Not Alone

Anxiety and depression lie. They tell you that you are alone, that no one understands, that nothing will ever get better. But those are lies.

You are not alone. You are seen. Your pain is real, but so is your ability to heal.

You deserve joy. You deserve peace. You deserve a life that feels worth living.

If you take nothing else from this chapter, take this: You are worthy of healing, and you do not have to carry this burden alone.

Chapter 9

Racism Is Bad For You

CHAPTER 9

Racism Is Bad For You

Racism is more than just a social injustice, it's a public health crisis. It's a constant, daily stressor that affects Black individuals physically, mentally, and emotionally. It leads to higher rates of anxiety, depression, high blood pressure, chronic disease, and even premature death.

For centuries, racism has been woven into the fabric of society, dictating where Black people can live, how they are treated in medical institutions, and whether they receive fair economic opportunities. But beyond the structural and economic oppression, racism literally makes people sick. The body does not differentiate between the stress of racism and other forms of trauma. Every racist experience, whether subtle or overt, activates the body's fight-or-flight response. Over time, this prolonged stress takes a heavy toll.

This chapter breaks down how racism affects health and well-being, and most importantly, how to fight back, not just in society, but within ourselves.

The Science of Racism and Stress

Racism triggers chronic stress, which activates the body's cortisol system, the hormone responsible for the fight-or-flight response. While this stress response is meant to protect us in short bursts, prolonged exposure to high stress levels leads to physical and mental deterioration.

1. Weathering: The Toll of Chronic Racism

Dr. Arline Geronimus coined the term weathering to describe how the constant stress of racism leads to early aging and poor health outcomes in Black people. This means that Black individuals, even when they take care of themselves, often experience:

- Higher rates of hypertension and heart disease due to chronic stress.
- Increased vulnerability to diabetes and stroke.
- Weaker immune systems, leading to greater susceptibility to illnesses.
- Shorter life expectancy compared to white counterparts.

The body quite literally wears down under the weight of discrimination, microaggressions, and societal exclusion.

2. Racial Trauma and Mental Health

Racial trauma is real. It's a psychological injury caused by repeated exposure to racism. This can happen through:

- Experiencing direct acts of racism (discrimination, police brutality, workplace exclusion).

- Seeing others experience racism (watching viral videos of racial violence).
- Historical trauma passed down through generations (family stories of segregation, slavery, or oppression).

Symptoms of racial trauma include:

- Chronic anxiety, hypervigilance, and panic attacks.
- Depression, hopelessness, and feelings of worthlessness.
- Anger, irritability, and emotional exhaustion.
- Difficulty trusting people, especially in predominantly white spaces.

The mind remembers racist experiences, even when the moment has passed. The stress doesn't just fade, it builds up over time, leading to a state of constant psychological distress.

The Impact of Racism on Black Health

1. Medical Racism: When the Healthcare System Fails Us

Black people are often dismissed, misdiagnosed, and undertreated in medical settings. Studies show that:

- Black patients normally receive less medication for pain because doctors believe they have a "higher pain tolerance."
- Black women pregnancy deaths are more likely to be 3x, or other relevant complications due to medical negligence.

- Black people are more likely to be misdiagnosed with schizophrenia instead of being treated for depression or anxiety.

This distrust of the medical system leads many Black individuals to avoid seeking medical care altogether, which only worsens health outcomes.

2. Workplace Racism: The Hidden Stressor

Racism in the workplace doesn't always look like outright discrimination. It often takes the form of:

- Being overlooked for promotions despite qualifications.
- Being expected to work harder than white colleagues to prove worth.
- Feeling the need to code-switch to be accepted.
- Experiencing microaggressions that make workspaces emotionally draining.

Workplace racism leads to high blood pressure, sleep disturbances, and burnout, making it a significant contributor to Black health disparities.

3. Environmental Racism: The Poisoning of Black Communities

There are always high chances that Black communities are exposed to pollution, toxic waste, and poor living conditions due to racist policies like redlining and gentrification. This leads to:

- Higher risks of asthma because of air pollution.

- Increased risk of cancer from industrial toxins in Black neighborhoods.
- Lack of access to clean water, fresh food, and quality healthcare.

Environmental racism ensures that Black communities suffer from preventable illnesses at alarming rates.

Fighting Back: Healing from the Effects of Racism

Racism is a systemic problem, but healing starts within. While we can't dismantle racism overnight, we can protect ourselves from its effects.

1. Protect Your Mental Health

- Limit exposure to racial trauma: Take breaks from watching distressing videos of racial violence.
- Find safe spaces: Surround yourself with people who uplift you.
- Seek therapy: A Black therapist or culturally competent counselor can help process racial trauma.
- Name your pain: Acknowledge that racism is affecting you instead of suppressing it.

2. Take Control of Your Physical Health

- Prioritize rest: Stress reduction is crucial. Sleep, meditate, and take mental health breaks.
- Advocate for yourself in medical settings: Get second opinions and demand proper care.

- Move your body: Exercise releases stress and counteracts the effects of chronic anxiety.
- Eat nourishing foods: A healthy diet strengthens the body against stress-related diseases.

3. Build Financial and Economic Power

- Support Black-owned businesses: Keep money circulating in the community.
- Invest in property and generational wealth: Break the cycle of financial oppression.
- Educate yourself on money management: Financial literacy is a tool for resistance.

4. Find Joy Despite It All

Racism tries to steal Black joy. Fighting back means reclaiming happiness in ways that nourish the soul.

- Celebrate Black culture through art, music, literature, and community.
- Engage in spiritual practices that ground and empower you.
- Laugh, dance, and rest without guilt, joy is resistance.

You Deserve to Thrive

Racism is designed to break spirits, shorten lives, and keep Black people in a constant state of struggle. But we are not meant to just survive, we are meant to thrive.

Healing from racism's effects is not just an individual journey, it's a collective one. When we care for ourselves, support each other, and push for systemic change, we reclaim our right to live freely, love fully, and exist unapologetically. You deserve peace. You deserve health. You deserve joy.

Chapter 10

Assimilate And Internalize Racism

CHAPTER 10

Assimilate And Internalize Racism

Racism doesn't just exist outside of us, it can take root within us. Internalized racism happens when oppressed people absorb the messages of inferiority that society projects onto them. It shapes how we see ourselves, how we treat each other, and how we navigate the world.

For many Black individuals, survival in a racist society has required assimilation, adapting to white cultural norms to avoid punishment, exclusion, or violence. From how we speak to how we dress, from the jobs we take to the way we wear our hair, the pressure to conform is constant. But at what cost?

This chapter examines how Black individuals and communities have been conditioned to internalize racism, the hidden costs of assimilation, and how to reclaim authentic Black identity without shame or fear.

What Is Internalized Racism?

Internalized racism is the unconscious acceptance of white supremacy's harmful narratives about Blackness. It manifests in beliefs such as:

- "Black people are lazy, violent, or unintelligent."
- "Dark skin is ugly, and light skin is better."
- "Speaking 'proper' English is the only way to sound educated."
- "Success means distancing myself from Black culture."
- "White spaces are more valuable than Black spaces."

These ideas don't come from within, they are imposed by a world that devalues Blackness. Over generations, these messages seep into our consciousness, shaping how we treat ourselves and each other.

Rejecting Your Own Culture – David's Struggle with Self-Acceptance

David, a 32-year-old marketing executive, grew up in a predominantly white neighborhood. From an early age, he noticed that being Black made him stand out in ways that felt uncomfortable.

At school, he was often the only Black student in his classes. Kids made jokes about his hair, his darker skin, and the way his mother spoke with an African accent. By the time he was a teenager, he had internalized the idea that being Black was something to be ashamed of.

Step 1: Trying to Fit In by Erasing Himself

To avoid standing out, David started distancing himself from anything that connected him to Black culture. He:

- Stopped speaking his parents' native language in public.
- Refused to eat African food at school to avoid being teased.
- Altered his speech to sound more "proper" and less like his Black peers.

His goal was to assimilate, to blend in so well that no one would see him as different. And for a while, it worked. His white peers accepted him, and he felt a sense of relief. But deep down, he always felt like he was performing.

Step 2: The Breaking Point

As an adult, David was highly successful in his career but deeply disconnected from himself. He had avoided friendships with other Black people, thinking it would make him seem "too Black."

It wasn't until he attended a company diversity meeting that something shifted. A colleague shared her experience with internalized racism, talking about how she used to reject her Blackness to fit in.

David felt exposed, she was describing exactly what he had been doing his whole life.

Step 3: Reclaim His Identity

David started questioning why he had spent years running from himself.

He began reconnecting with his culture by:

- Learning about African history and Black excellence.
- Embracing his natural hair instead of keeping it cut short to "look professional."
- Building relationships with Black colleagues and friends who understood his struggles.

Through this journey, David realized that accepting himself fully was the true path to belonging, not assimilation.

The Roots of Internalized Racism

Internalized racism is a direct result of colonization, slavery, segregation, and systemic oppression. When a group is oppressed for long enough, some members begin to police each other to survive. This leads to:

- Respectability politics: The belief that behaving "properly" (by white standards) will earn Black people respect.
- Colorism: Preference for lighter skin tones due to European beauty standards.
- Division within the Black community: Classism, elitism, and the rejection of certain forms of Blackness.
- Self-doubt and self-hate: Feeling not good enough, not smart enough, or not worthy of success.

These beliefs are not natural. They are taught, and they can be unlearned.

The Pressure to Assimilate: A Survival Tactic

Assimilation is the act of adopting the dominant culture's norms, values, and behaviors to fit in. For Black people, this often means:

- Code-switching, changing speech patterns or behavior in white spaces.
- Downplaying racial identity to avoid making others uncomfortable.
- Rejecting Black cultural expressions (hairstyles, slang, music) to be seen as "professional."
- Seeking validation from white institutions while devaluing Black spaces.

Code-Switching to Survive – Ayanna's Battle with Double Consciousness

Ayanna, a 25-year-old law student, was well aware that how she presented herself impacted how people treated her. Growing up, she learned to code-switch, adapting her speech, tone, and mannerisms based on her environment. In professional settings, she spoke in a polished, neutral tone. Around her Black friends, she felt free to be herself.

But after years of code-switching, she started feeling exhausted and disconnected from her true identity.

Step 1: The Unspoken Rules of Code-Switching

As a student at a prestigious law school, Ayanna was often one of the few Black people in the room. She knew that:

- Speaking too passionately might make her seem "aggressive."
- Wearing natural hairstyles could be seen as "unprofessional."
- Using AAVE (African American Vernacular English) could lead to judgment.

She played by these unspoken rules because she believed it was necessary to succeed.

Step 2: Realizing the Toll It Took

One day, after a long study session, a classmate told her, "You're so articulate for a Black girl."

Ayanna forced a polite smile, but inside, she was furious. Why did being articulate have to be a surprise?

She realized that no matter how much she code-switched, she was still being judged through a racial lens. This made her question whether playing by these rules was truly worth it.

Step 3: Embracing Authenticity

Instead of continuing to shrink herself, Ayanna decided to:

- Wear her natural hair in professional settings without feeling the need to conform.
- Speak in her natural tone without fear of being "too Black" for certain spaces.
- Challenge microaggressions directly, instead of laughing them off.

She discovered that she could be successful without sacrificing her identity. She no longer saw code-switching as a survival strategy but as a choice she controlled, not something she was forced into.

Many Black individuals assimilate out of necessity, to get jobs, to avoid discrimination, or even to stay safe. But assimilation comes at a high cost.

The Emotional Toll of Assimilation

Assimilation forces Black people to constantly monitor themselves, leading to:

- Chronic stress and anxiety.
- Imposter syndrome, feeling like a fraud despite success.
- Exhaustion from constantly "performing" a version of oneself.
- Guilt for feeling disconnected from one's cultural roots.

At some point, many realize that no amount of assimilation will make them truly "accepted" in a society built on racism. That realization can be painful, but also liberating.

Reclaiming Black Identity: Break Free from Internalized Racism

Healing from internalized racism begins with unlearning the lies and embracing Black identity fully. Let's see how:

1. Deprogram Your Mind

- Question negative beliefs about Blackness. Who taught you to think that way? Is it true?
- Learn Black history beyond slavery. Study African civilizations, Black intellectuals, and revolutionary movements.
- Recognize and reject colorism. All Black skin tones are beautiful and worthy.
- Celebrate Black language, music, art, and cultural expressions. They are valid and valuable.

2. Stop Seeking Validation from White Institutions

- Your worth is not defined by whiteness. You don't need to prove yourself by mimicking white success.
- Black excellence exists in all forms, not just those approved by white standards.
- You don't have to be "the only Black person in the room" to feel accomplished. Invest in Black spaces.

3. Let Go of Respectability Politics

- You don't owe the world a "polite" version of yourself to be treated with respect.
- Black hairstyles, dialects, and cultural practices are not unprofessional.
- Blackness is diverse. There's no single way to "be Black."

4. Embrace Black Community and Healing Spaces

- Find Black mentors, therapists, and role models who affirm your identity.
- Support Black businesses, media, and movements that uplift the community.
- Have honest conversations about internalized racism with friends and family.

5. Give Yourself Permission to Be Fully Black, Unapologetically

- You don't have to shrink yourself to make others comfortable.
- You don't have to explain or justify your Blackness to anyone.
- You are enough, as you are, without changing for anyone's approval.

Unlearning Internalized Racism – Malik's Journey to Self-Love

Malik, a 19-year-old college student, grew up hearing negative stereotypes about Black people, not just from outsiders, but from within his own community.

His uncles would say things like, "Black people are lazy, that's why we struggle." His teachers assumed he wouldn't do well in school. His white classmates treated him as if he was naturally less intelligent.

After years of hearing these messages, he started believing them.

Step 1: Recognizing Internalized Racism

Malik didn't realize how deeply he had absorbed these ideas until one day, in a class discussion, he criticized other Black students for talking about systemic racism.

He said, "Maybe if we worked harder, we wouldn't have these problems."

A classmate challenged him: "Do you really think our struggles are because we're lazy? Or have you just been taught to believe that?"

This question shook Malik to his core. He realized that he had been repeating the same stereotypes used to oppress his people.

Step 2: Educating Himself

Determined to unlearn these toxic beliefs, Malik:

- Read books about Black history and systemic racism.
- Listened to podcasts about Black empowerment.
- Had conversations with mentors who helped him see his own worth.

He realized that Black people weren't struggling because they were lazy, but because of centuries of systemic barriers.

Step 3: Rebuilding a Healthy Self-Image

Malik began replacing harmful beliefs with affirmations of self-worth:

- "My Blackness is powerful, not a weakness."
- "I am just as capable and intelligent as anyone else."

- "Black culture is rich, brilliant, and worth celebrating."

Instead of internalizing racism, he embraced Black pride. He went from seeing his race as a limitation to recognizing it as a source of strength.

Freedom from the Need to Assimilate

Internalized racism thrives in silence and shame. The more we talk about it, the more we heal from it.

Rejecting assimilation doesn't mean rejecting success. It means defining success on your own terms, without betraying your identity.

True freedom is not just fighting racism in society. It's fighting the racism we've been taught to believe about ourselves.

You don't have to assimilate to be worthy. You are already enough.

Chapter 11

Explore And Expand Meaningful Blackness

CHAPTER 11

Explore And Expand Meaningful Blackness

Blackness is not a monolith. It is expansive, dynamic, and deeply rooted in history, culture, and resilience. However, the effects of colonization, racism, and internalized oppression have led many to question what it truly means to be Black. Is Blackness defined by struggle? Is it limited to certain behaviors, speech patterns, or cultural markers? Or can it be something broader, something deeply personal, yet universally powerful?

This chapter is about reclaiming Blackness on our own terms, free from the restrictive definitions imposed by society. It is about exploring Black identity with pride, depth, and nuance, and expanding it beyond survival into a source of power, joy, and self-determination.

Defining Blackness for Yourself

The world often tries to define Blackness in limited ways:

- Too Black vs. Not Black Enough: Some feel pressure to prove their Blackness by conforming to cultural stereotypes, while others feel disconnected because they don't fit mainstream expectations.
- Struggle as Identity: Blackness is often tied to pain and oppression, as if suffering is a requirement for authenticity.
- Respectability Politics: Society rewards Black individuals who conform to white cultural norms, reinforcing the idea that certain expressions of Blackness are more acceptable than others.

But Blackness cannot be reduced to a checklist. It is not something to prove, it is something to live.

The Expansiveness of Black Identity

Blackness is:

- Cultural and historical, rooted in traditions, languages, and customs that span Africa, the Caribbean, the Americas, and beyond.
- Spiritual and ancestral, linked to deep legacies of resilience, creativity, and innovation.
- Intellectual and philosophical, embodied by scholars, revolutionaries, artists, and thinkers who have shaped the world.
- A personal experience, unique to each individual, shaped by family, environment, and self-discovery.

By embracing its expansiveness, we allow ourselves to explore and define Blackness on our own terms.

Break Free from Limited Views of Blackness

1. Let Go of the Idea That Blackness Must Equal Struggle

- Yes, we have endured oppression, but Blackness is more than pain.
- Blackness is also joy, love, beauty, and resilience.
- We must allow ourselves to thrive, not just survive.

2. Challenge the "Right" and "Wrong" Ways to Be Black

- There is no single way to be Black. Whether you love hip-hop or classical music, whether you speak in African American Vernacular English (AAVE) or not, your Blackness is valid.
- Black nerds, Black athletes, Black revolutionaries, Black scientists, Black artists, all expressions of Blackness matter.

3. Embrace Black Global Connections

- Blackness is not just African American, it is international.
- Explore the rich histories and cultures of Black people across the diaspora.
- Learn about African civilizations, Caribbean revolutions, and Afro-Latinx contributions to the world.

4. Reclaim and Celebrate African Roots

- Colonization severed many Black people from African history and identity. Reconnecting is a powerful act of resistance.
- Learn African history beyond slavery, explore the greatness of civilizations like Mali, Kush, and Ethiopia.
- Embrace African cultural practices, music, fashion, and spirituality.

Black Joy and Self-Expression as Resistance

1. Finding Joy in Blackness

- Joy is a radical act in a world that tries to break us.
- Celebrating Black culture, food, music, and traditions is a way of reclaiming power.
- Dancing, laughing, resting, and enjoying life unapologetically are revolutionary.

2. Honoring Black Creativity and Innovation

- Black people have shaped music, fashion, art, and literature globally.
- Explore Black creatives and support Black-owned media and businesses.
- Your self-expression, whether through art, writing, or activism, is a continuation of Black brilliance.

3. Building Meaningful Black Communities

- Blackness thrives in community. Find spaces where you can connect, heal, and grow.

- Support Black businesses, movements, and educational initiatives.
- Teach younger generations the fullness of Black history and identity.

Here are two examples.

EXAMPLE: Malcolm X's Journey to Meaningful Blackness

One of the most profound examples of exploring and expanding meaningful Blackness is the life transformation of Malcolm X. His journey serves as a powerful case study of how embracing identity can lead to personal empowerment and societal impact.

Early Struggles and Identity Confusion

Malcolm X, born Malcolm Little, who grew up in a society that constantly devalued Blackness. As a child, he witnessed racism's destructive force firsthand, his father was likely murdered by white supremacists, and his mother was institutionalized due to severe emotional distress. This left young Malcolm feeling abandoned, lost, and disconnected from any real understanding of his cultural roots.

During his teenage years and early adulthood, Malcolm sought identity in ways that many Black individuals in oppressed communities do, through crime, survival tactics, and self-rejection. He straightened his hair to look more "acceptable," distanced himself from his African heritage, and even engaged in criminal activities that ultimately led to his incarceration.

The Awakening: Knowledge as a Tool To Reclaim Blackness

Prison became a turning point for Malcolm X. He immersed himself in reading, devouring books on history, philosophy, and race relations. Through self-education and exposure to the Nation of Islam, Malcolm realized how deeply systemic racism had influenced his sense of self-worth. He reclaimed his Black identity by rejecting the slave name "Little" and embracing "X," symbolizing his lost African heritage.

Expanding His Understanding of Blackness

Initially, Malcolm X's identity transformation was rooted in racial separatism, as he believed that Black people could only find dignity through complete independence from white society. However, his pilgrimage to Mecca in 1964 challenged his earlier beliefs. Seeing people of all races practicing Islam together made him realize that meaningful Blackness was not about hatred or isolation, it was about self-respect, unity, and self-determination.

By the time of his assassination in 1965, Malcolm had become a symbol of Black empowerment, global solidarity, and intellectual awakening. His story illustrates that exploring meaningful Blackness is a lifelong journey, one that involves questioning societal narratives, educating oneself, embracing cultural pride, and evolving beyond initial understandings.

Malcolm X's transformation is a blueprint for those struggling to find and embrace their own identity. His life shows that:

- Cultural knowledge is key to understanding and reclaiming Black identity.
- Self-reinvention is possible, no matter how lost one feels.
- Blackness is dynamic and evolves over time, shaped by experience, knowledge, and personal growth.

For anyone wondering how to navigate their own identity struggles, Malcolm's journey offers a powerful testament that Blackness is something to be explored, expanded, and embraced on one's own terms.

PRACTICAL EXAMPLE: A Modern-Day Journey to Embracing Blackness

To make this more relatable, let's consider a modern-day example of someone struggling with their Black identity and how they can actively explore and expand meaningful Blackness.

Meet Jordan: A Young Black Professional in Search of Identity

Jordan is a 27-year-old African American working in the corporate world. Growing up in a predominantly white suburb, Jordan often felt disconnected from Black culture. In school, classmates would joke that Jordan was "Black on the outside, white on the inside" because of their interests in alternative music and formal speech. This led Jordan to question their Black identity, feeling alienated from both Black and white spaces.

After entering the workforce, Jordan faced subtle microaggressions, colleagues would act surprised at their intelligence, and superiors suggested they "loosen up" to be more approachable. Jordan felt pressure to conform to white corporate expectations while also feeling a void in cultural identity.

Step 1: Self-Education and Cultural Awareness

One day, Jordan stumbled upon a podcast discussing Black identity, history, and the struggles of assimilation.

Intrigued, Jordan began researching topics like:

- The African diaspora and how history shaped modern Black experiences.
- Code-switching and how many Black professionals navigate dual identities.
- The Black arts movement and how creative expression fuels cultural pride.

Reading books like "The Souls of Black Folk" by W.E.B. Du Bois and watching documentaries about Black history helped

Jordan see that there is no "right way" to be Black, Blackness is diverse and layered.

Step 2: Connecting with the Black Community

Realizing that a sense of community was missing, Jordan took steps to engage with Black culture and people more intentionally:

- Attended local Black-owned business events to support entrepreneurship.
- Joined a professional Black networking group, meeting peers who shared similar experiences.
- Visited Black cultural spaces like museums, poetry readings, and historically Black colleges (HBCU) events.

Slowly, Jordan felt more rooted in Blackness, not by changing who they were, but by expanding their understanding of what being Black could mean.

Step 3: Rejecting the Need for Validation

A key moment in Jordan's journey was rejecting the "Black enough" narrative. Instead of trying to fit into a single version of Black identity, Jordan embraced personal authenticity. Whether enjoying hip-hop and jazz or indie rock and classical music, Jordan realized that Blackness was not about external approval, it was about self-acceptance and cultural awareness.

Step 4: Using Blackness as a Source of Strength

As Jordan became more comfortable in their identity, confidence grew. No longer suppressing cultural expressions at work, Jordan started advocating for diversity initiatives and mentoring younger Black employees. Understanding and expanding their Blackness gave Jordan a stronger voice in every area of life.

The Path to Meaningful Blackness is Personal

Jordan's journey shows that embracing meaningful Blackness is not about conforming to stereotypes, it's about:

- Educating yourself on your history and heritage.
- Surrounding yourself with positive Black influences and community.
- Defining what Blackness means to YOU, not what society tells you it should be.

Jordan's story proves that there are many ways to embrace and expand Black identity, it's a lifelong journey of growth, learning, and self-acceptance.

Your Blackness, Your Terms

Being Black is not about fitting into a mold. It is about embracing the full depth and richness of who you are. You do not have to prove your Blackness to anyone.

Blackness is yours to define, explore, and expand, without limits, without fear, and without apology.

Chapter 12

Heal Through Community-Based Solutions

CHAPTER 12

Heal Through Community-Based Solutions

Healing from Post-Traumatic Slave Syndrome (PTSS) is not just a personal journey, it is a collective effort. For centuries, Black communities have thrived through shared strength, cultural traditions, and mutual support despite systemic oppression, economic marginalization, and generational trauma. The concept of community-based healing is deeply rooted in African traditions, where the well-being of one is tied to the well-being of all.

This chapter explores the power of community healing and how rebuilding collective support systems can break cycles of trauma and create lasting empowerment. By reviving these traditions and adapting them to modern challenges, we can foster emotional, economic, and social well-being within our communities.

Why Healing as a Community is Essential

Trauma does not happen in isolation, and neither should healing. Individual therapy and self-care are crucial, but they are not enough. A person can only heal fully when their environment supports and nurtures their growth.

1. Collective Trauma Requires Collective Healing

- Black communities have endured centuries of oppression, systemic racism, and economic disenfranchisement. These experiences have left a lasting imprint, often manifesting as internalized oppression, distrust, and generational wounds.
- When an entire community is impacted by racial violence, poverty, or discrimination, addressing these issues at the individual level alone is not sufficient.
- Healing must involve restoring community trust, rebuilding social connections, and reclaiming cultural identity.

2. Individual Healing is Harder in Isolation

- Loneliness and alienation increase stress, anxiety, and depression.
- People struggling with PTSS often internalize their pain because they feel like no one else understands.
- When healing is approached collectively, individuals see that they are not alone, others share similar struggles and can offer support, wisdom, and encouragement.

3. Cultural Healing is Passed Down Through Generations

- Healing is not just about recovering from the past, it's about preserving and passing on cultural knowledge to future generations.
- Strong communities teach children resilience, self-worth, and collective responsibility, ensuring that healing continues beyond just one lifetime.

Healing Through Community – Jasmine's Path to Collective Healing

Jasmine, a 40-year-old social worker, had spent most of her life prioritizing others' needs over her own. She worked tirelessly in underserved communities, advocating for at-risk youth and single mothers. But over time, she burned out, emotionally, mentally, and spiritually.

Despite helping others heal, Jasmine rarely focused on her own healing journey. She felt isolated, exhausted, and began questioning whether she could continue in her career.

Step 1: Seeking Support Within a Community Circle

One day, a colleague invited her to a community healing circle, a gathering where Black individuals could share their struggles, uplift one another, and practice collective healing. At first, Jasmine hesitated. She had always been the strong one; opening up felt uncomfortable.

However, when she finally attended, she experienced something powerful, the safety of being seen and heard without judgment. Others shared similar struggles with burnout, racial trauma, and emotional exhaustion. For the first time, Jasmine realized she wasn't alone.

Step 2: Learning and Practicing Restorative Healing

Through the community circle, Jasmine was introduced to restorative practices rooted in African traditions, such as:

- Talking circles, where participants openly discuss their feelings.
- Breathing and meditation sessions, designed to release stress and trauma.
- Intergenerational mentorship, where elders offer wisdom and younger members provide fresh perspectives.

The healing circle became Jasmine's safe space, a place where she could be vulnerable and find strength in collective care.

Step 3: Becoming an Advocate for Community Healing

Feeling renewed, Jasmine decided to bring healing-centered practices into her professional work. She organized mental health workshops, self-care retreats, and peer support groups for social workers and activists.

By prioritizing community-based healing, she saw firsthand how powerful collective support and shared experiences could be. Jasmine no longer felt like she had to carry the burden alone, her healing was intertwined with the healing of her community.

Final Thoughts

These three examples highlight the diverse ways Black individuals can heal through community-based solutions:

- Lisa's journey shows how economic healing and financial literacy can break generational cycles.
- Marcus's story demonstrates the power of art and music as healing tools for emotional expression.
- Jasmine's experience proves that collective healing through community support is essential for long-term emotional well-being.

Healing is not a solo mission, it thrives in shared spaces, cultural traditions, and mutual support systems. When Black communities come together to empower, uplift, and heal each other, they create pathways for resilience, joy, and transformation.

By understanding the importance of collective healing, we can take active steps to rebuild our communities in ways that promote growth, resilience, and empowerment.

Rebuilding Safe Spaces for Healing

Healing requires safe spaces, places where people feel heard, valued, and protected from judgment. Historically, Black communities have relied on churches, family gatherings, and cultural organizations as spaces of safety and resilience. However, systemic oppression and modern societal shifts have eroded many of these safe spaces.

1. Physical Spaces for Healing

- Community Centers: Spaces where people can access mental health services, financial literacy workshops, and peer support groups.
- Cultural Hubs: Spaces dedicated to music, art, storytelling, and African heritage as a means of healing.
- Healing Circles: Small group gatherings where individuals can share their stories, express emotions, and find support.
- Gardening and Farming Spaces: Reconnecting with the land through community gardens can be a form of healing and empowerment.

2. Emotional and Psychological Safe Spaces

- Removing Stigma Around Mental Health: Community leaders must work to normalize therapy, emotional expression, and vulnerability.
- Encouraging Honest Conversations: People must feel comfortable discussing trauma, grief, and personal struggles without fear of judgment.
- Protecting Mental and Emotional Boundaries: Communities should discourage toxic behaviors, gossip, and invalidation of people's emotions.

By actively creating and protecting safe spaces, we allow healing to happen without fear or shame.

The Role of Mentorship and Eldership in Healing

One of the most powerful tools for healing in the Black community has always been mentorship. Elders have historically played a key role in guiding younger generations, sharing wisdom, and ensuring cultural knowledge is preserved. However, many of these mentorship structures have been disrupted due to family separation, economic displacement, and mass incarceration.

1. Why Mentorship is Important

- Reconnecting with Cultural Roots: Elders can pass down traditions, languages, and values that have been lost due to systemic oppression.
- Providing Emotional Support: Many young people need positive role models who can provide guidance for facing life challenges.
- Teaching Resilience: Mentors can help youth navigate racism, economic hardship, and identity struggles with confidence.

2. How to Rebuild Mentorship Networks

- Community Meetups: Organizing intergenerational gatherings where elders share their experiences with youth.
- Support Circles: Creating groups for young men and women to discuss identity, self-worth, relationships, and mental health.

- Skill-Sharing Programs: Teaching financial literacy, entrepreneurship, and life skills that empower younger generations.

When elders and youth work together, healing becomes a cycle of strength rather than a cycle of trauma.

Economic Healing Through Collective Empowerment

Economic trauma is one of the deepest wounds left by slavery, segregation, and systemic racism. Many Black communities still suffer from disinvestment, redlining, and job discrimination, making financial stress a major barrier to healing. However, community-based economic solutions can change this reality.

1. Financial Stability as a Form of Healing

- Money stress is a major trigger for anxiety, depression, and trauma responses.
- Communities that invest in financial education, cooperative economics, and Black-owned businesses build generational wealth and collective stability.

2. Solutions for Economic Empowerment

Cooperative Economics (Group Investments):

Community members pool money to invest in housing, businesses, and education.

This reduces financial risk and creates shared prosperity.

Prioritizing Black-Owned Businesses:
Buying from Black businesses keeps money circulating within the community, strengthening financial independence.
Teaching Financial Literacy:
Communities should offer classes on budgeting, investing, and debt management.

Economic Healing – Lisa's Journey to Financial Empowerment

Lisa, a 35-year-old single mother, had always struggled financially. Raised in a low-income neighborhood, she witnessed firsthand the impact of generational poverty and financial trauma. Growing up, money was a source of stress, and discussions about savings or investments were almost nonexistent. Her family lived paycheck to paycheck, and credit card debt was a usual part of life.

After college, Lisa found herself in a similar cycle. Despite earning a stable income, she struggled with financial anxiety and a scarcity mindset, constantly fearing she would never have enough. She often felt guilty spending money on herself and was overwhelmed by debt, making it difficult to plan for the future.

Step 1: Financial Literacy and Mindset Shift

Lisa's turning point came when she attended a financial wellness workshop hosted by a Black-owned community organization. The workshop covered essential financial topics like budgeting, credit repair, investing, and wealth-building strategies. For the first time, Lisa learned that her financial struggles weren't just personal failings, they were deeply rooted in systemic barriers that had long affected Black communities.

She began reading books like "The Black Tax" by Shawn Rochester and listening to podcasts about economic empowerment. This helped her shift her mindset from one of scarcity to abundance and strategy.

Step 2: Creating a Plan for Stability

Determined to break free from financial PTSD, Lisa took proactive steps:

- Opened a high-yield savings account and started saving consistently.
- Paid off high-interest debt using the debt snowball method.
- Joined a community investment group, where members pooled money to invest in local Black-owned businesses.

This support system helped Lisa stay accountable and build generational wealth rather than just survive financially.

Step 3: Giving Back to the Community

As Lisa gained financial confidence, she began teaching financial literacy to others in her community. She volunteered at high schools to educate students about budgeting and investing early. Eventually, she started a side business as a financial coach, helping Black families break cycles of financial trauma and build generational wealth.

Lisa's story proves that economic healing is possible with knowledge, strategic planning, and community support. By prioritizing financial education and collective wealth-building, she not only transformed her own life but empowered others to do the same.

By focusing on economic healing, we lay the foundation for mental and emotional stability within our communities.

Healing Through Art, Music, and Storytelling

Art has always been a powerful form of resistance and healing in Black culture. From slave spirituals to hip-hop, music and storytelling have been used to process trauma, inspire change, and build community resilience.

1. The Healing Power of Storytelling

- Sharing personal and ancestral stories validates pain, honors history, and fosters collective strength.
- Community storytelling events allow people to express emotions, learn from elders, and connect with shared experiences.

2. Music as a Therapeutic Tool

- Music has always been an outlet for emotional release and spiritual healing.

- Gospel, blues, jazz, and hip-hop all carry deep messages of survival, hope, and empowerment.

3. Artistic Expression as a Form of Therapy

- Dance, poetry, and painting provide non-verbal ways to process trauma.
- Art therapy programs in community centers and schools can empower youth to express emotions safely.

Healing Through Art and Music – Marcus Finds Healing in Creative Expression

Marcus, a 29-year-old veteran, struggled with anxiety, PTSD, and depression after returning home from military service. He found it difficult to open up about his emotions, and traditional therapy didn't seem to help. He often felt disconnected from his community and numb to the world around him.

Step 1: Discovering Art as an Outlet

One evening, while scrolling through social media, Marcus came across a local Black art therapy program. Skeptical at first, he decided to attend one session. The facilitator, a Black artist and mental health advocate, encouraged attendees to express their emotions through painting, music, and poetry.

At first, Marcus struggled to let go. But as he dipped his brush into vibrant colors and let his emotions flow onto the canvas, he felt a sense of release he hadn't experienced before.

Through art, he could communicate feelings he couldn't put into words.

Step 2: Music as a Healing Tool

In addition to painting, Marcus was introduced to drumming and rhythm therapy. He learned that African drumming has been used for centuries as a form of spiritual and emotional healing. The deep, resonant beats helped him regulate his breathing, calm his racing thoughts, and feel connected to something larger than himself.

Step 3: Building a Supportive Creative Community

Encouraged by his progress, Marcus began attending weekly art and music therapy sessions. He formed bonds with other Black men and women who also used creative expression as a way to heal from trauma. Eventually, he started writing and performing spoken-word poetry, using his voice to tell his story and inspire others.

Marcus's journey demonstrates that healing doesn't always come from traditional methods. Creative expression, whether through painting, music, dance, or poetry, offers an alternative path to emotional recovery, especially for those who struggle to verbalize their pain.

Today, Marcus mentors young Black artists, teaching them how to use creativity as a tool for emotional resilience. His story shows that art and music are more than entertainment, they are powerful forms of self-care, self-expression, and healing.

By embracing art and storytelling, communities create a collective space for emotional healing and cultural pride.

Reclaim the Power of Collective Healing

Healing from PTSS is not just about personal recovery, it's about reviving the strength of entire communities. By rebuilding safe spaces, mentoring youth, fostering economic stability, and embracing cultural healing, we create a foundation for true transformation.

We must move beyond survival and create a future where Black communities thrive, heal, and empower future generations.

Healing is not just possible, it is necessary. And we must do it together.

Chapter 13

Make The Most Of Your Spiritual Resourcefulness

CHAPTER 13

Make The Most Of Your Spiritual Resourcefulness

The Power of Spiritual Resourcefulness

Spirituality has long been a cornerstone of resilience and healing for Black communities. In times of enslavement, segregation, systemic oppression, and personal struggle, faith, prayer, meditation, and other spiritual practices have provided a refuge, a source of strength when all else seemed lost.

However, spirituality is not just about religion. Spiritual resourcefulness is about tapping into a deep well of inner strength, wisdom, and connection, whether that comes from faith, ancestral traditions, nature, or personal introspection. It is the ability to draw upon unseen yet deeply felt sources of power to navigate life's challenges, heal from trauma, and create a fulfilling existence.

In this chapter, we will explore how spiritual resourcefulness can be a powerful tool for healing from Post-Traumatic Slave Syndrome (PTSS) and generational trauma, how we can reclaim our spiritual traditions, and how to apply spiritual principles to foster resilience, purpose, and peace.

Reclaim Spirituality Beyond Oppression

For many in the Black community, spirituality has been a double-edged sword. While it has been a source of empowerment, it has also been used as a tool of control and oppression. Colonizers and enslavers manipulated religious teachings to justify slavery and subjugation. However, within that same religious framework, Black people found ways to reinterpret faith as a means of liberation.

1. From Control to Empowerment

- Enslaved Africans brought with them rich spiritual traditions that were forcibly stripped away and replaced with European Christianity. However, rather than accept it passively, many reinterpreted Christian teachings to reflect their own struggles, seeing figures like Moses as a symbol of Black liberation.
- Over time, Black-led churches became not just places of worship but centers of community, activism, and social change.
- Today, many are exploring African traditional religions (ATR) such as Ifá, Vodun, and Kemetic spirituality to reconnect with ancestral wisdom.

2. Expanding the Definition of Spirituality

- Spirituality does not have to be religious. Some find deep spiritual meaning in meditation, nature, art, or human connection.
- Spirituality is deeply personal. Whether through prayer, ritual, reflection, or creative expression, each person must find what nourishes their soul.
- Healing spiritual wounds. Many people carry religious trauma, feeling disconnected from spirituality because of past experiences with rigid, judgmental, or oppressive religious institutions. Reclaiming spiritual resourcefulness is about healing and finding a belief system that supports your well-being.

Healing Through Spiritual Connection

1. Spirituality as a Tool for Healing Trauma

PTSS, intergenerational trauma, and racial oppression have caused deep wounds in the Black community. Spirituality can be a profound healing tool for addressing these wounds:

- Faith as a Coping Mechanism: Many who face depression, anxiety, and despair find solace in prayer, scripture, or sacred texts that offer wisdom and hope.
- Meditation and Mindfulness: Rooted in African, Eastern, and Indigenous traditions, mindfulness practices help calm the nervous system, regulate emotions, and foster inner peace.

- Rituals for Emotional Healing: Lighting candles, journaling, burning sage, or engaging in personal ceremonies can create sacred spaces for healing.
- Speaking with Ancestors: Many cultures believe in the continued presence of ancestors as guides and protectors, offering wisdom and intercession in times of need.

2. Community and Collective Healing

Spirituality is not just personal, it is collective. Many Black communities heal through communal worship, prayer circles, healing circles, and spiritual gatherings. These spaces provide:

- Validation of shared experiences, knowing you are not alone.
- Opportunities to release grief and pain in safe, sacred settings.
- Collective strength to combat oppression and injustice.

Integrating Ancestral Wisdom into Daily Life

1. Understanding African Spirituality

Many Black people have been disconnected from their ancestral spiritual traditions due to colonization, forced conversion, and systemic erasure. Reconnecting with these traditions can offer a profound sense of identity and empowerment.

- Ancestral Veneration: Honoring those who came before us through prayer, altars, or rituals can provide guidance and protection.
- African Proverbial Wisdom: Many African cultures use proverbs to pass down wisdom. Phrases like "If you want to go fast, go alone. If you want to go far, go together" teach the importance of community.
- Traditional Healing Practices: Herbal medicine, energy work, and spiritual cleansings (such as using Florida Water, sage, or palo santo) can be incorporated into healing routines.

2. Spiritual Practices for Daily Resilience

- Morning Affirmations: Start each day with affirmations of strength and purpose. ("I am worthy, I am resilient, I am protected.")
- Journaling and Reflection: Writing down thoughts, prayers, or meditations can provide clarity and emotional release.
- Meditation and Breathwork: These techniques help regulate stress, anxiety, and trauma responses.
- Rituals for Protection: Many cultures use rituals such as wearing protective symbols (ankhs, crystals, beads) or speaking protective words before leaving home.

Faith in Action: Using Spirituality for Social Change

1. Spirituality and Activism

Throughout history, Black liberation movements have been deeply tied to spiritual beliefs. Figures including Malcolm X, Harriet Tubman, and Martin Luther King Jr., all saw their work as divinely guided. Their faith was not passive, it was a call to action.

- Prayer and Protest: Churches and mosques have historically been organizing centers for civil rights activism.
- Spiritual Resistance: Enslaved Africans used coded spiritual songs ("Wade in the Water") as messages for escape.
- Faith-Based Social Movements: Organizations like Black Liberation Theology challenge traditional religious narratives to advocate for justice and equity.

2. Balancing Spirituality with Practical Action

- Faith should empower action, not replace it. While prayer and meditation are powerful, they should be accompanied by tangible efforts toward self-improvement and community betterment.
- Avoid using spirituality to bypass emotional or psychological struggles, healing requires both spiritual practices and practical steps like therapy, financial literacy, and self-care.

Overcoming Spiritual Blocks

1. Deconstructing Religious Trauma

Many people have negative experiences with religion due to:

- Judgmental teachings that promote fear and shame.
- Religious institutions that uphold oppression rather than liberation.
- Conflicts between traditional beliefs and modern personal growth.

Healing from religious trauma involves:

- Allowing yourself to redefine spirituality on your terms.
- Separating harmful doctrine from spiritual truths that empower you.
- Exploring alternative spiritual practices that resonate with your soul.

2. Avoiding Spiritual Bypassing

Spiritual bypassing is when people use spirituality to avoid dealing with real-world issues, such as trauma, systemic racism, or mental health challenges. Examples include:

- "Just pray about it" instead of seeking therapy.
- Blaming struggles on "karma" rather than addressing systemic injustices.
- Using forgiveness as a reason to ignore harm and avoid accountability.

True spiritual resourcefulness requires balance, faith and action, prayer and therapy, meditation and movement.

Faith and Resilience – Elijah's Journey to Spiritual Strength

Elijah, a 42-year-old father of three, had always been a man of faith, but life had tested him in ways he never expected. Growing up in a strong Black church community, he had been taught that faith could get him through anything. But when he lost his job during an economic downturn, followed by the sudden death of his younger brother, Elijah found himself spiraling into depression.

For the first time in his life, he questioned everything: his purpose, his ability to provide for his family, and even his faith. He stopped attending church, isolated himself from loved ones, and wrestled with deep feelings of hopelessness. He had always been the one offering spiritual encouragement to others, but now, he didn't know how to receive the support he needed.

Step 1: Reconnecting with Faith in a New Way

One evening, while scrolling online, Elijah came across a virtual faith-based support group for Black men struggling with grief and life challenges. Skeptical but desperate, he joined a session. To his surprise, it wasn't just a space for quoting scriptures, it was a brotherhood where men openly discussed mental health, self-doubt, and emotional pain through a spiritual lens.

Hearing others voice the struggles he had been silently carrying gave him permission to be vulnerable. He realized that faith wasn't just about being strong, it was also about leaning on community and allowing himself to be supported.

Step 2: Rebuilding His Spiritual Practice

With renewed hope, Elijah began incorporating small spiritual practices into his daily life:

- Journaling his prayers to process emotions.
- Listening to gospel and uplifting music to reset his mindset.
- Meditating on scripture not just for knowledge but for healing.

He started attending church again but also expanded his understanding of spirituality beyond just Sunday services.

Step 3: Using Faith to Empower Others

With time, Elijah not only healed but became a mentor in the same support group that had saved him. He helped other men see that faith isn't about having all the answers, it's about walking the journey even when the path isn't clear.

Through his spiritual resilience, Elijah realized that true faith isn't about avoiding hardship; it's about finding the strength to rise again, even after being knocked down.

Spirituality Beyond Religion – Ayana's Path to Holistic Healing

Ayana, a 30-year-old wellness coach, had never been deeply religious, but she always felt a strong connection to spirituality, nature, and ancestral wisdom. Raised in a culturally mixed household, she was exposed to both traditional African spiritual practices and modern mindfulness techniques.

However, after experiencing a painful breakup and workplace burnout, Ayana found herself emotionally drained and disconnected from herself. She knew she needed healing but didn't know where to start.

Step 1: Exploring Spirituality Beyond Traditional Religion

Rather than forcing herself into religious spaces that didn't resonate, Ayana explored holistic spiritual practices that honored both her African roots and her personal beliefs:

- She visited an elder in her community who taught her about the importance of ancestral veneration and prayer.
- She started daily meditation and breathwork, using these practices to ground herself.
- She embraced affirmations and manifestation, rewriting negative thoughts and embracing self-love.

Through these practices, Ayana realized that spirituality is not just about external rituals, it's about alignment, balance, and inner peace.

Step 2: Healing Through Nature and Ancestral Wisdom

Seeking deeper healing, Ayana took a solo trip to a nature retreat hosted by Black wellness practitioners. There, she engaged in forest therapy, a practice of reconnecting with nature to heal stress and trauma.

She also learned about traditional African spiritual healing techniques such as:

- Libation rituals, where she honored her ancestors by offering water and gratitude.
- Herbal healing, using plants like sage and lavender for cleansing and relaxation.
- Sound healing, using African drumming and chanting to realign her energy.

Through these experiences, she felt a deep reconnection with herself and her roots, realizing that spirituality could be personal, fluid, and freeing.

Step 3: Sharing Spiritual Healing with Others

Feeling transformed, Ayana integrated these practices into her coaching business. She began offering wellness retreats, guided meditation sessions, and ancestral healing workshops for Black women seeking spiritual renewal.

Through her journey, Ayana discovered that spirituality doesn't have to fit into a box, it can be a deeply personal, evolving relationship with oneself, community, and ancestral wisdom.

These two stories show that spiritual resourcefulness takes different forms:

- Elijah's story shows how faith and community can restore hope and purpose.
- Ayana's journey proves that spirituality can be deeply personal and rooted in self-discovery.

Both highlight that healing comes when we embrace spiritual tools that align with our authentic selves.

Your Spirituality, Your Power

Spiritual resourcefulness is about reclaiming, reshaping, and expanding the role of spirituality in your life.

Whether through faith, ancestral traditions, meditation, or personal reflection, spirituality can be a profound source of healing, strength, and guidance.

You do not have to conform to oppressive religious structures to be spiritual. Your path is yours to create.

You have the right to explore your ancestry, traditions, and inner power.

Your spirituality is a tool, not just for survival, but for thriving. By making the most of your spiritual resourcefulness, you step into a deeper sense of purpose, resilience, and wholeness. This is your journey, walk it with strength, intention, and unwavering belief in yourself.

Chapter 14

Being Genuine

CHAPTER 14

Being Genuine

One of the most difficult yet vital steps in the healing journey is the willingness to ask for help. For many individuals, especially within the Black community, acknowledging the need for help can be seen as a vulnerability, a weakness, or even a failure. However, true strength lies in recognizing when support is necessary and taking steps to seek it out.

Being genuine about needing help is not just about asking for assistance, it's about creating space for vulnerability, opening yourself up to support, and giving yourself permission to prioritize your well-being. This chapter delves into why asking for help can be transformative, the barriers that prevent many of us from doing so, and how to create a culture of possible care and support that fosters growth, healing, and empowerment.

The Power of Vulnerability

For many, vulnerability feels like a heavy burden to carry. It's often associated with weakness, shame, or a lack of independence. In a society that often expects people to "pull themselves up by their bootstraps," admitting that we need help can feel counterproductive. Yet, vulnerability, the willingness to acknowledge our emotional, mental, or physical struggles, has immense power.

1. Vulnerability is a Gateway to Healing

When we allow ourselves to be vulnerable, we create the space to begin the healing process. Healing cannot happen in isolation or under the pressure of pretending to be okay when we are not. Vulnerability is the bridge between suffering in silence and receiving the support we need to begin healing.

In the context of Post-Traumatic Slave Syndrome (PTSS), many Black individuals have carried the weight of collective and individual trauma for generations. The pressure to be resilient and strong often masks the underlying emotional and psychological damage. But vulnerability offers a path to reclaiming our humanity, admitting that we are not invincible and that seeking help is an act of strength, not weakness.

2. The Collective Nature of Healing

Healing is not a solitary act; it is a communal process. The idea that we must face our struggles alone often stems from deep-rooted societal messages that equate independence with strength. Yet, the reality is that no one can heal in isolation. Humans are social creatures, and we thrive when we are connected to others. Vulnerability allows us to reach out to others, connect, and build the networks of support we need.

In the Black community, communal healing has always been a cornerstone of survival and resilience. From the strength of extended families to the support offered by faith-based organizations and activist movements, community care has been essential in navigating the trials and tribulations of systemic racism and oppression. Recognizing the power of vulnerability and being genuine about our need for help can unlock these communal networks and further support our healing journeys.

Why We Struggle to Ask for Help

Despite the transformative power of vulnerability, many individuals find it difficult to ask for help. Several factors, cultural, societal, and personal, contribute to this struggle. The key to understanding these barriers is to overcome them and foster a culture of mutual care.

1. The Stigma Around Mental Health

Historically, mental health issues have been stigmatized within Black communities. For many, mental health struggles were seen as a form of weakness or something to be ashamed of. This stigma often arises from a combination of societal misconceptions, generational trauma, and the pressure to "keep moving forward" despite personal struggles.

In addition, therapy and counseling were often perceived as luxuries, only accessible to the privileged. Many individuals may not have had the resources or knowledge to access mental health support. It's essential not to stay silent around mental health in creating a space in which individuals can conduct open discussions on their struggles and seek help without fear of judgment.

2. The Legacy of Resilience

Black communities have long been celebrated for their resilience in the face of adversity. Due to the legacy of slavery and the Civil Rights Movement, survival has often been synonymous with strength. This historical context has led many to adopt a mindset of "just keep going", to avoid showing vulnerability, to endure without complaint, and to reject help in favor of self-reliance.

While resilience is a strength, it can also become a double-edged sword. The constant need to be strong can overshadow the need for care and support. For many, admitting weakness or vulnerability feels like betraying that legacy of survival. Yet, true strength is in knowing when to lean on others for help and when to say, "I cannot do this alone."

3. Fear of Rejection or Burdening Others

For some, asking for help is met with a connected fear that they will be judged, rejected, or become a burden to others. This fear can stem from a lifetime of not receiving support when it was needed most, leading to a lack of trust in others.

However, rejection is not the norm. In healthy, supportive communities, there is a reciprocal understanding that we are all interconnected. Just as we help others, we should allow ourselves the grace to receive help. Asking for help does not make you a burden, it makes you human.

How to Begin Asking for Help

The process of asking for help requires intention, courage, and trust. The first step in this journey is acknowledging that it is okay to need help. Once that mindset is established, it becomes easier to reach out to others and create a plan for healing and growth. Here are some strategies for beginning this process.

1. Start by Acknowledging the Need

The first step in asking for help is to acknowledge to yourself that you need it. This may sound simple, but for many, it is the hardest part of the process. It requires confronting feelings of shame, guilt, or fear. Start by being kind to yourself and accepting that you are allowed to need help.

Journaling, self-reflection, and meditation can all be useful tools for recognizing where you need support. Whether it's emotional, mental, financial, or physical, being honest with yourself is the foundation of any healing process.

2. Identify the Type of Help You Need

Help can come in many forms, emotional support, professional therapy, financial assistance, or even just someone to listen. Take time to reflect on what type of help you need most. Are you struggling with depression and need therapy? Are you feeling isolated and need companionship? Do you need financial assistance to help with medical bills or basic needs?

Being clear about the type of help you need allows you to focus on reaching out to the right people or organizations that can provide that support. Clarity is key to ensuring that your needs are met.

3. Reach Out to Trusted Individuals or Professionals

Once you've identified the type of help you need, reach out to those who can provide it. This might be a family member, a close friend, a community leader, or a professional therapist. It's important to reach out to individuals who are trustworthy, supportive, and non-judgmental. If you feel hesitant about approaching a person directly, consider starting with a message or letter, or even seeking out online resources or support groups.

For mental health needs, reaching out to a therapist or counselor is a crucial step. Therapy is not a sign of weakness, it is a tool for growth and self-discovery.

4. Be Open to Receiving Help

Asking for help is one thing; accepting it is another.

It's important to be open to receiving help without guilt or hesitation. Often, people resist help because they fear being perceived as weak, or they feel unworthy of the care being offered. But help is a gift. By accepting help, you allow others the opportunity to contribute to your healing process and strengthen your connection with them.

5. Build a Support Network

Healing is not a one-time event, it's a journey. Build a support network that includes individuals who can offer ongoing support, encouragement, and accountability. This might involve close friends, family, professionals, or community groups. Having a network of people who understand your struggles and are willing to support you through them is invaluable.

Examples:

Break the Silence – Malcolm's Journey to Therapy

Malcolm, a 38-year-old father of two, had spent years bottling up his emotions. Raised in a household where men were expected to be strong and silent, he learned early on that vulnerability was a sign of weakness. His father never spoke about feelings, and whenever Malcolm showed sadness as a child, he was told to "man up" or "stop acting soft."

As an adult, Malcolm carried these beliefs into his relationships. He prided himself on being the provider and keeping his struggles to himself. But beneath the surface, he was dealing with crippling anxiety, mood swings, and moments of deep sadness that he couldn't explain.

Step 1: Hitting a Breaking Point

One day, after a heated argument with his wife, Malcolm's emotions boiled over. He felt overwhelmed, like he was drowning in stress. That night, he didn't sleep, staring at the ceiling, realizing that he was exhausted, physically, mentally, and emotionally.

He had spent so long pretending to be okay that he had no idea how to admit that he needed help. He feared being judged, but at the same time, he knew that something had to change.

Step 2: Taking the First Step Toward Help

A few weeks later, Malcolm saw an ad for a Black men's mental health initiative offering free virtual therapy sessions. At first, he hesitated. Therapy felt like something "other people" did, not him. But something in him told him to try.

During his first session, Malcolm struggled to open up. He answered questions with short, vague responses. But his therapist, a Black man with a calm and understanding presence, didn't push, he just listened.

Over time, Malcolm felt safe enough to talk about his childhood, his fears of failure, and the pressure he carried as a Black man.

Step 3: Realizing That Asking for Help is Strength

Through therapy, Malcolm learned:

- His emotions weren't a weakness, they were a natural human experience.

- He didn’t have to carry everything alone, seeking help made him stronger, not weaker.
- Breaking generational cycles of silence could help his children grow up feeling safe to express their emotions.

Malcolm now encourages his friends to talk openly about mental health and normalizes therapy in his community. He realized that asking for help isn’t giving up, it’s fighting for yourself in the best way possible.

Building a Support Network – Nia’s Path to Emotional Healing

Nia, a 27-year-old graduate student, had always been the "strong friend." The one who gave advice, supported everyone, and never showed weakness. She believed that as long as she kept pushing forward, everything would be fine.

But behind closed doors, she was mentally drained. She constantly felt anxious, had trouble sleeping, and was emotionally exhausted. She had people around her, but she felt alone in her struggles.

Step 1: Realizing That Strength is in Connection

One evening, after a particularly stressful day, Nia's best friend, Tasha, noticed something was wrong. "You always ask how everyone else is doing," Tasha said. "But when was the last time you let someone ask about you?"

Nia shrugged it off at first, saying she was just tired. But later, she realized she never let herself lean on others. She had built walls around her emotions, afraid of burdening people with her problems.

That night, she took a deep breath and sent a message to Tasha: "Actually, I haven't been okay for a while."

Step 2: Allowing Herself to Receive Help

Tasha immediately called her, and for the first time, Nia opened up about everything. The stress, the anxiety, the fear of being a burden. Instead of judgment, Tasha responded with understanding and support.

Encouraged by this, Nia started confiding in a few other trusted friends. She realized that the people in her life wanted to be there for her, they just didn't know she needed help.

Step 3: Finding Healing in Community

With a newfound support system, Nia took additional steps:

- She joined a Black women's healing circle, where she could share experiences with others who understood.
- She started journaling her emotions, helping her process feelings she had suppressed for years.
- She learned to set boundaries, saying no to things that drained her and prioritizing self-care.

Over time, Nia felt lighter, freer, and more emotionally connected. She realized that strength isn't about handling everything alone, it's about knowing when to reach out.

Now, she helps other women recognize that being vulnerable is a superpower, not a flaw.

The above two stories highlight that seeking help is not a sign of failure, it's an act of courage:

- Malcolm's story shows that breaking the silence about mental health can lead to profound healing.
- Nia's journey proves that leaning on community can provide the emotional support needed to heal.

Both emphasize that no one has to suffer in silence, help is there, but we must be willing to accept it.

Creating a Culture of Support

While it's important to learn how to ask for help as an individual, it is equally essential to create a culture of support within our communities. A healthy, thriving community is one in which individuals feel safe to be vulnerable, ask for help, and offer assistance to others.

We can foster a culture of support by:

- Promoting open conversations about overall well-being and mental health.
- Breaking down the stigma surrounding seeking help.
- Encouraging intergenerational care, elders providing wisdom and youth offering fresh perspectives.
- Creating mutual support networks where people can both give and receive help.

Strength in Asking for Help

In the journey to heal from trauma and reclaim our well-being, the act of asking for help is not just a necessity, it is an act of strength. The ability to admit we need help and seek it out demonstrates profound self-awareness and self-compassion.

It's time to embrace vulnerability, challenge the stigma around seeking help, and empower ourselves and others to prioritize healing. The road to recovery and growth is not walked alone, we are all in this together

Chapter 15

How To Make Therapy Work

CHAPTER 15

How To Make Therapy Work

Therapy can be a transformative experience, but only when approached with the right mindset and expectations. Many people find it difficult to seek professional help due to stigma, past negative experiences, or a belief that therapy "won't work" for them. The truth is, therapy is a tool, one that requires active participation, self-awareness, and commitment to be truly effective.

This chapter is about demystifying therapy, helping you understand how to make it work for your specific needs, and giving you strategies to ensure your healing journey is as impactful as possible.

Why Therapy Matters

For many, the idea of therapy is associated with crisis, something you seek out only when everything has fallen apart. In reality, therapy is a preventative and empowering resource. Just like we visit doctors for regular checkups, therapy should be viewed as a way to maintain and strengthen mental and emotional well-being before things reach a breaking point.

Therapy can help you:

- Process past trauma and break negative cycles.
- Develop coping mechanisms for stress, anxiety, and depression.
- Improve relationships by understanding communication patterns.
- Unpack limiting beliefs that stem from cultural conditioning or personal experiences.
- Reclaim your personal narrative by reshaping harmful thought patterns.

Overcoming Skepticism – Jamal's First Steps into Therapy

Jamal, a 35-year-old construction worker, had always been skeptical about therapy. Raised in a family that believed "what happens in the house stays in the house," he had been taught that handling your problems alone was just part of life.

For years, he carried the weight of childhood trauma, relationship struggles, and financial stress without ever considering professional help. When his best friend suggested therapy after noticing Jamal's increased drinking and anger outbursts, Jamal dismissed it.

"Man, therapy's just for rich people or weak folks. I don't need to talk to a stranger about my problems."

But deep down, he knew he wasn't okay. The stress was getting worse, and he had no healthy way to release his emotions.

Step 1: Taking a Small Step

After weeks of hesitation, Jamal looked up therapy options online. He found a local clinic that offered low-cost virtual sessions for Black men. Still doubtful, he booked an appointment, telling himself he'd just check it out once and never go back.

During his first session, Jamal barely spoke. He gave one-word answers and avoided eye contact. But his therapist didn't push, he simply listened. At the end, he told Jamal:

"You don't have to say everything today. Just showing up is enough for now."

Step 2: Learning to Open Up

By the third session, Jamal started sharing small things, his childhood, his stress at work, and how he struggled to communicate with his girlfriend without getting defensive. He realized therapy wasn't about being weak, it was about learning new tools to handle life differently.

His therapist helped him:

- Recognize unhealthy coping habits (like drinking to numb emotions).
- Practice expressing emotions without shutting down.
- Understand that seeking help is strength, not failure.

Step 3: Seeing Real Changes

Six months in, Jamal noticed real change. He no longer exploded in anger over small things. He started setting boundaries at work and in relationships. Most importantly, he realized that therapy wasn't about being broken, it was about growing.

If you've struggled with PTSS, intergenerational trauma, or personal hardships, therapy can provide the tools needed to navigate these challenges in a healthy and productive way.

Finding the Right Therapist

The effectiveness of therapy often depends on finding the right therapist, someone whose approach, experience, and personality align with your needs.

1. Look for Cultural Competence

Not all therapists understand the complexities of historical trauma, racial identity, and systemic oppression. If you are dealing with PTSS or related struggles, it is crucial to find a therapist who:

- Acknowledges the role of systemic oppression in mental health.
- Understands cultural trauma and the impact of racism.
- Can offer affirming and relevant guidance.

2. Choose the Right Therapy Style

Therapy is not one-size-fits-all. Different approaches work for different individuals, so it's important to explore the right fit:

- Cognitive Behavioral Therapy (CBT): Helps challenge and reframe negative thought patterns.
- Psychodynamic Therapy: Addresses past experiences and how they shape present behavior.
- Somatic Therapy: Focuses on trauma stored in the body through movement and mindfulness.
- Narrative Therapy: Empowers you to rewrite your personal story.
- Group Therapy: Provides healing through shared experiences and collective support.

If you've tried therapy before and felt it wasn't helpful, it could be that the approach wasn't right for you rather than therapy itself being ineffective.

3. Don't Be Afraid to Switch Therapists

If, after a few sessions, you feel unheard, dismissed, or uncomfortable, it's okay to look for another therapist. Therapy is about YOU, and you deserve a professional who truly supports your healing process.

Finding the Right Therapist – Maya's Journey to Culturally Competent Care

Maya, a 28-year-old law student, had tried therapy before, but it never worked for her. Her first therapist was kind but didn't understand her experiences as a Black woman. She'd say things like "I don't see race" or downplay Maya's workplace struggles as if they weren't real.

Feeling misunderstood, Maya stopped going after three sessions.

"Maybe therapy just isn't for me," she thought.

Step 1: Realizing the Importance of Cultural Fit

After months of struggling with stress and imposter syndrome, Maya decided to give therapy another shot, but this time, on her terms. She specifically searched for Black female therapists and found one who specialized in racial trauma and women's mental health.

Step 2: Feeling Seen for the First Time

From the first session, the difference was clear. Her new therapist didn't dismiss her concerns, she validated them.

When Maya talked about microaggressions at school, her therapist didn't brush it off, she gave her tools to navigate them. When Maya expressed feeling exhausted by societal pressures, her therapist reminded her that Black women often feel this way due to historical and cultural expectations.

For the first time, Maya felt seen and heard.

Step 3: Learning How to Make Therapy Work for Her

Through therapy, Maya learned that finding the right therapist is just as important as going in the first place. She also discovered that:

- She had the right to switch therapists if one wasn't a good fit.
- Therapy wasn't just venting, it was about learning skills to cope and grow.
- Black mental health matters, and finding someone who understands cultural nuances is life-changing.

With her new therapist, Maya felt empowered. She finally had a space where she could be unapologetically herself, and that made all the difference.

How to Get the Most Out of Therapy

Simply attending therapy sessions is not enough, you have to be an active participant in the process. How to ensure therapy works for you:

1. Be Honest, Even When It's Uncomfortable

Therapy is a space for truth.

The more open and honest you are about your struggles, the more effective the process will be. Holding back information out of fear, shame, or discomfort can slow down your progress.

- If something is painful to talk about, acknowledge it instead of avoiding it.
- If you're unsure how you feel, express your uncertainty rather than pretending to have all the answers.

- If you disagree with your therapist's suggestions, speak up and discuss it.

Vulnerability is not weakness, it's the key to genuine healing.

2. Set Clear Goals

Therapy works best when you know what you want to achieve. Before starting, ask yourself:

- What specific issues am I struggling with?
- What patterns do I want to break?
- What emotions do I want to better understand?

Setting clear goals, whether it's reducing anxiety, improving relationships, or healing past trauma, helps direct the focus of your therapy sessions.

3. Be Patient with the Process

Therapy is not an overnight fix. It takes time to unpack deeply rooted issues, and progress often happens in layers. Some sessions might feel like breakthroughs, while others might feel slow or even frustrating.

Trust the process, and grow at your own pace. They say that healing is not linear and setbacks are also a natural part of progress.

4. Apply What You Learn Outside of Therapy

Therapy does not end when the session is over.

To make it truly effective, you have to actively apply the insights and strategies you learn in real life.

- Practice the coping techniques your therapist teaches you.

- Engage in self-reflection between sessions.
- Journal about your emotions and experiences to track progress.
- Communicate openly with friends and family about what you're working on.

Therapy is not just about understanding your struggles, it's about actively transforming your life outside of the therapy room.

Overcoming Barriers to Therapy

1. Overcoming Stigma

Many communities, especially Black communities, have been conditioned to view therapy as unnecessary or a sign of weakness. This stigma is deeply rooted in historical mistrust of medical systems, but it's crucial to break this mindset.

Seeking therapy does not mean you are "broken", it means you are strong enough to prioritize your mental and emotional well-being.

2. Affording Therapy

Therapy maybe expensive but affordable options are also available:

- Look for sliding-scale therapists who adjust fees based on income.
- Seek out community-based mental health services that offer free or low-cost sessions.
- Check if your employer or insurance plan covers therapy.

- Consider online therapy platforms, which are often more affordable than in-person sessions.

3. Finding Time for Therapy

Your busy schedules can be a hurdle to prioritize therapy, but mental health is just as important as physical health. If necessary:

- Schedule sessions at flexible times, such as evenings or weekends.
- Consider virtual therapy if in-person visits are too time-consuming.
- Start with biweekly or monthly sessions if weekly sessions feel overwhelming.

Committing to the Process – DeShawn's Breakthrough in Therapy

DeShawn, a 41-year-old entrepreneur, had been in therapy for six months but felt stuck. At first, he was excited, he showed up, answered the therapist's questions, and even took notes. But after a while, he started feeling like nothing was changing. "I'm talking, but I still feel the same. Maybe therapy just doesn't work for me."

Step 1: Understanding That Change Takes Time

DeShawn's therapist helped him understand that therapy isn't instant relief, it's a long-term process. Just like physical fitness, mental and emotional strength require consistent effort. Together, they made a structured plan:

- Journaling after every session to track his progress.
- Practicing the coping strategies learned in therapy outside of sessions.
- Checking in every few weeks to assess what was working and what wasn't.

Step 2: Doing the Work Outside of Sessions

One of DeShawn's biggest struggles was dealing with childhood wounds. His therapist introduced inner child work, where he reflected on past experiences that shaped his fears and behaviors.

At first, it was uncomfortable. But once he committed, he started noticing patterns, how his fear of failure stemmed from his father's criticism, or how his avoidance of deep relationships was tied to past heartbreak.

By actively applying what he learned in therapy, instead of just talking about it, DeShawn finally started to see real change.

Step 3: Embracing Therapy as a Lifelong Tool

After a year in therapy, DeShawn had:

- Stronger emotional awareness, he could identify his triggers before reacting.
- Better relationships, he communicated more openly instead of shutting down.
- A toolkit for life, coping mechanisms he could rely on, even after therapy ended.

DeShawn's story shows that therapy isn't a quick fix, it's an investment in yourself. The more effort you put in, the more you gain.

Therapy is a powerful tool, but like any tool, it only works if you commit to using it properly.

Your healing is worth the time investment.

Therapy as a Tool for Liberation

Therapy is not just about coping, it's about transformation. It is a tool that helps unpack generational trauma, challenge harmful beliefs, and build emotional resilience.

If you approach therapy with openness, patience, and a commitment to growth, it can be one of the most life-changing decisions you make.

No matter where you are in your journey, remember this: you deserve healing. You deserve peace. You deserve a life free from the weight of past pain.

Therapy is not about fixing what is "wrong" with you, it's about helping you step into your fullest potential.

So when you need it, let it work for you.

Chapter 16

Apply New And Improved Tools To Overcome Stress

CHAPTER 16

Apply New And Improved Tools To Overcome Stress

Stress is an unavoidable part of life, but for individuals affected by Post-Traumatic Slave Syndrome (PTSS), the burden can be far heavier. Beyond the everyday stressors of work, relationships, and finances, those carrying the weight of generational trauma experience stress at a deeper level, one that is influenced by historical oppression, systemic inequality, and cultural displacement. When stress becomes chronic, it has lasting effects on the mind, body, and spirit, leading to emotional exhaustion, physical ailments, and mental health struggles.

The good news? Stress does not have to dictate your life. By understanding its roots and applying new, effective strategies, you can take control of your well-being and develop resilience to life challenges. This chapter explores practical, evidence-based tools to help you manage stress in a way that is sustainable, culturally relevant, and empowering.

Recognizing the Hidden Impact of Stress

Many people think of stress as simply feeling overwhelmed or exhausted. However, stress operates on multiple levels, physiological, emotional, and psychological, often without us even realizing its full impact.

How Stress Manifests in the Body

When faced with stress, the body activates its fight-or-flight response, releasing hormones like cortisol and adrenaline. While this response is helpful in emergencies, chronic activation leads to problems such as:

- Weakened immune system – makes you more vulnerable to illness.
- High blood pressure and heart disease – due to prolonged tension in the body.
- Muscle pain and headaches – caused by ongoing physical stress.
- Disruptions in sleep and digestion – leading to fatigue and gut health issues.

How Stress Manifests in the Mind

Chronic stress also affects mental well-being, often leading to:

- Racing thoughts and overthinking.
- Irritability, mood swings, or sudden emotional outbursts.
- Feelings of hopelessness or detachment.

- Struggles with concentration or decision-making.

For those carrying generational trauma, stress can also trigger feelings of unworthiness, fear of failure, or deep-seated self-doubt, all of which contribute to cycles of anxiety and burnout.

The key to Break free? Recognizing these symptoms early and applying targeted strategies to address them.

Tools for Managing and Overcoming Stress

While there is no one-size-fits-all approach to stress relief, holistic, culturally relevant tools can help reduce its impact and restore a sense of balance. Here are five essential strategies to help you take charge of your stress and reclaim your peace of mind.

1. Grounding Techniques to Reset the Nervous System

When stress takes over, grounding techniques help bring your mind and body back to the present moment, calming anxiety and reducing tension.

How to Practice Grounding:

- 5-4-3-2-1 Method: Identify 5 things you see, and 4 things you can touch, 3-things you hear, and 2 things you smell, and 1 thing you taste. This simple exercise immediately shifts focus from stress to the present.
- Temperature Therapy: Hold a piece of ice, splash cold water on your face, or take a warm bath. Sudden

temperature changes can shock the nervous system out of panic mode and into relaxation.

- Deep Breathing Exercises: You need to inhale deeply for 4 seconds, now hold for 4 seconds, and finally exhale slowly for 6 seconds. The parasympathetic nervous system activates which tells your body that it's safe to relax.

Grounding is especially effective for interrupting negative thought spirals and calming stress before it escalates.

2. Mindfulness and Meditation for Emotional Balance

Mindfulness helps reduce stress by bringing awareness to the present moment without judgment. Meditation strengthens this practice by training the mind to stay calm, even in the face of stress.

How to Use Mindfulness and Meditation:

- Mindful Eating: Instead of rushing through meals, slow down and savor each bite. Pay attention to taste, texture, and smell.
- Walking Meditation: Take a slow, intentional walk, focusing on each step, breath, and the environment around you.
- Guided Meditation: Use apps or videos with guided meditations, especially those designed for healing from racial trauma or generational stress.

By practicing mindfulness regularly, you reduce reactivity, making it easier to handle stress without feeling overwhelmed.

3. Physical Movement as a Stress Release

Stress often gets trapped in the body, leading to muscle tension, fatigue, and physical discomfort. Moving your body is one of the most effective ways to release built-up stress and improve mental clarity.

How to Use Movement for Stress Relief:

- Rhythmic Exercise: Activities like dancing, drumming, or even simple head nodding help sync the body and mind, reducing stress.
- Stretching and Yoga: Gentle stretching or yoga movements restore balance to the nervous system by releasing tight muscles.
- Strength Training: Engaging in resistance exercises or lifting weights can turn stress into energy, making you feel more empowered.

The key is to find movements that feel natural and enjoyable, whether that's a structured workout or simply swaying to your favorite music at home.

4. Cognitive Restructuring: Reframing Negative Thoughts

Our thoughts shape our reality, and when stress is high, negative thoughts often take control. Cognitive restructuring helps identify and challenge self-defeating beliefs before they cause harm.

How to Reframe Negative Thoughts:

- Identify Automatic Negative Thoughts (ANTs): When stress triggers thoughts like "I'll never succeed" or "I'm not good enough", write them down.
- Challenge the Thought: Ask yourself, "Is this thought based on facts or just fear?"
- Replace with a More Balanced Thought: Instead of "I can't do this," say, "This is difficult, but I have overcome challenges before."

This method helps break the cycle of stress-induced self-doubt and creates a healthier mental environment.

5. The Power of Community and Social Support

One of the greatest antidotes to stress is connection. Being part of a supportive community reminds you that you are not alone, and that healing happens best when shared.

Ways to Cultivate Support:

- Join Cultural or Faith-Based Groups: Spaces that celebrate shared experiences and heritage provide comfort and strength.
- Engage in Collective Healing Practices: Group meditation, storytelling circles, or community discussions help release stress through shared expression.
- Seek Professional Guidance When Needed: Therapy, counseling, or support groups can offer valuable tools and strategies tailored to your needs.

Strong social connections reduce stress, increase resilience, and provide the encouragement needed to keep moving forward.

Break the Cycle of Burnout – Jason's Journey to Mental Balance

Jason, a 38-year-old software engineer, was a classic workaholic. He prided himself on grinding hard, staying up late, and always being available for his company.

For years, he convinced himself that exhaustion was just part of success. But beneath the surface, his body and mind were screaming for help.

Step 1: Ignoring the Warning Signs

At first, Jason's stress showed up in small ways:

- Constant headaches and muscle tension.
- Irritability with family and friends.
- A feeling of never truly resting, even on weekends.

He dismissed these as minor issues, until his doctor warned him that his blood pressure was dangerously high.

Step 2: Realizing the Need for Change

One day, Jason collapsed at his desk. It wasn't a heart attack, but it was a severe anxiety attack.

His doctor told him bluntly: "If you don't find better ways to manage your stress, your body will force you to stop."

That was the wake-up call he needed.

Step 3: Applying New Stress-Relief Tools

Determined to break the cycle of burnout, Jason started making real changes:

1. Creating Clear Work-Life Boundaries
    - He stopped checking emails after 7 PM and turned off notifications.
    - He took real lunch breaks instead of eating at his desk.
2. Using Physical Activity to Release Stress
    - He started boxing three times a week, releasing pent-up frustration.
    - He swapped coffee for hydration and better sleep.
3. Practicing Stress-Management Techniques
    - He learned deep breathing exercises to manage stress in the moment.
    - He kept a gratitude journal to shift his focus from pressure to progress.

Step 4: Seeing the Difference

Within months, Jason felt like a different person:

- He had more energy.
- His stress levels dropped dramatically.
- He finally enjoyed life again, without guilt.

His story proves that stress doesn't have to control you, if you're willing to take control first.

Heal Through Mindfulness and Community – Tanisha's Path to Inner Peace

Tanisha, a 45-year-old single mother of three, had been carrying the weight of the world for years.

Between work, parenting, and financial struggles, she had no time for herself. She felt like she was drowning in stress, but asking for help wasn't an option in her mind.

Step 1: The Silent Suffering of Stress

Tanisha was always on edge:

- She barely slept, waking up every few hours worrying about bills.
- She felt emotionally drained, snapping at her kids even though she loved them.
- She pushed through the pain, thinking self-care was a luxury she couldn't afford.

She didn't realize how much stress was controlling her life, until she hit rock bottom.

Step 2: Finding Healing Through Mindfulness

One day, her best friend signed her up for a free meditation class. At first, Tanisha resisted.

"I don't have time for this."

But something happened in that first session. For the first time in years, she sat still, focused on her breath, and felt a deep sense of calm.

Step 3: Making Stress Management a Daily Practice

Seeing how powerful a few minutes of mindfulness could be, Tanisha started applying small changes to her daily life:

1. Morning Mindfulness
   - Instead of waking up to stress, she started each day with 5 minutes of deep breathing.
   - She wrote down three things she was grateful for, shifting her focus from struggle to strength.
2. Using Community for Support
   - She joined a local single-moms' support group, realizing she wasn't alone.
   - She let herself ask for help, accepting that strength isn't about doing everything alone.
3. Letting Go of Unnecessary Stress
   - She learned to say no to things that drained her.
   - She replaced negative self-talk with affirmations of self-worth.

Step 4: Feeling Free Again

Tanisha's stress didn't disappear overnight, but she no longer let it control her.

- She felt lighter, mentally and emotionally.
- She had tools to manage stress instead of letting it build up.
- Her kids noticed the change, and so did she.

Her journey proves that healing from stress isn't about escaping it, it's about learning how to handle it in a way that gives you peace.

Taking Control of Your Stress

Stress may be inevitable, but suffering from it doesn't have to be. By integrating these tools, grounding, mindfulness, movement, cognitive reframing, and social connection, you create a personalized stress-management system that supports your overall well-being.

Most importantly, healing from PTSS and generational trauma requires compassion for yourself. You are allowed to feel overwhelmed, but you also have the power to choose tools that help you heal, grow, and thrive.

Each small step toward stress relief is a step toward freedom, resilience, and self-empowerment, one that reclaims not only your personal peace but also the legacy of strength that generations before you have fought to preserve.

Chapter 17

Claim Your Truths And Make Change Possible

CHAPTER 17

Claim Your Truths And Make Change Possible

The Power of Owning Your Truth

Change begins with acknowledgment. Before transformation can take place, whether on a personal, cultural, or societal level, we must first claim our truths. This means facing the realities of our history, our struggles, and the ways in which generational trauma has shaped us. For individuals and communities affected by Post-Traumatic Slave Syndrome (PTSS), this process can be both liberating and challenging.

Claiming the truth of your experiences does not mean dwelling in pain. Instead, it is about understanding where you come from, recognizing the forces that have shaped you, and using that knowledge to move forward with clarity, strength, and purpose. In this chapter, we will explore why truth-telling is essential for healing, how to break free from the narratives imposed on us, and how embracing your authentic self can lead to meaningful personal and collective change.

Why Claiming Your Truths Is Necessary for Healing

Many people go through life carrying unspoken burdens, whether from childhood trauma, systemic oppression, or personal hardships. These truths, when left unacknowledged, create internal conflict, leading to the feelings of self-doubt, confusion, and emotional distress.

For those impacted by PTSS, claiming personal and historical truths is particularly important because it allows for:

- Recognition of Hidden Wounds: Acknowledging how generational trauma has affected mental health, relationships, and self-perception.
- Breaking the Cycle of Silence: Many families and communities avoid discussing difficult truths, but silence only prolongs suffering. Speaking out is the first step toward healing.
- Releasing Shame and Guilt: Internalized oppression often leads to self-blame. Understanding history helps shift the blame from oneself to the systemic forces that created these struggles.
- Reclaiming Personal and Cultural Identity: Recognizing and embracing your true self, free from societal expectations or imposed identities.

Until these truths are faced, real and lasting change remains out of reach.

The Impact of Denying Your Truth

Ignoring or suppressing your truths can manifest in various ways:

1. Emotional Suppression and Mental Health Struggles

When painful experiences are buried rather than addressed, they often resurface as anxiety, depression, or anger. Many people develop unhealthy coping mechanisms, such as substance abuse, emotional detachment, or even self-sabotage.

2. Generational Cycles of Trauma

If past wounds are not acknowledged, they are unintentionally passed down. For example, if a parent never addresses their own childhood trauma, they may unconsciously recreate similar patterns in their own children's lives.

3. Living a False Identity

Many individuals, especially those from marginalized communities, feel pressure to assimilate into dominant societal norms, often at the expense of their own authenticity. This leads to a disconnect between who they truly are and the identity they present to the world.

4. Stagnation and Lack of Growth

Without facing and accepting truth, it becomes difficult to move forward. Suppressed pain keeps people stuck in toxic relationships, unfulfilling careers, and cycles of self-doubt. Denial may feel like a protective shield, but in reality, it creates deeper wounds.

Steps to Claiming Your Truths and Using Them for Change

The process of truth-claiming is deeply personal and requires intentional effort. Below are practical steps that can help guide this journey.

1. Identify the Truths You Have Been Avoiding

Self-reflection is the starting point. Ask yourself:

- What personal experiences have I been hesitant to acknowledge?
- What societal narratives have shaped my beliefs about myself?
- Are there aspects of my family history or cultural identity that I have ignored?
- How have past experiences influenced my self-worth and decision-making?

Journaling is a powerful tool in this stage. Writing your thoughts uncensored helps bring buried truths to the surface.

2. Confront the Fear of Truth-Telling

Many people avoid acknowledging difficult truths because of fear, fear of judgment, rejection, or the emotional pain that may come with it. However, avoiding the truth does not make it disappear.

How to Overcome This Fear:

- Acknowledge that discomfort is temporary.
  Growth often comes with discomfort, but facing the truth leads to long-term relief.
- Seek safe spaces for expression. Whether through therapy, trusted friends, or support groups, sharing

your truth in a non-judgmental environment makes it easier.

- Recognize that truth empowers. The more you accept your reality, the stronger and more confident you become.

3. Reject False Narratives Imposed by Society

History has created many false narratives about marginalized communities, stories that portray them as inferior, undeserving, or broken. Many people internalize these messages, leading to self-doubt and insecurity.

Ways to Challenge and Reject False Narratives:

- Educate yourself on history beyond mainstream perspectives.
- Understanding historical truths gives context to current struggles and debunks myths.
- Surround yourself with empowering representations. Consume books, media, and cultural content that reflect your true identity with dignity and strength.
- Affirm your own worth. Challenge self-limiting beliefs with daily affirmations like "I am enough," "I am worthy of love and success," and "My story is valuable."

By dismantling harmful narratives, you create space for self-acceptance and empowerment.

4. Speak Your Truth – Even When It Feels Difficult

Truth has power, but only when it is expressed. Once you acknowledge your truths, the next step is to share them in ways that inspire growth and healing.

Ways to Express Your Truth:

- Have honest conversations with loved ones. Break cycles of silence by speaking openly about issues that have been avoided.
- Engage in storytelling. Whether through writing, art, music, or public speaking, sharing your journey helps others who may be struggling in similar ways.
- Advocate for social change. Speaking out against systemic injustices helps create collective transformation.

Even small acts of truth-telling create ripples of change.

5. Use Truth as a Tool for Personal and Collective Growth

Truth is not just about reflection, it is about action.

Once you have claimed your truths, use them as a guide to shape the future you want.

Ways to Use Truth for Growth:

- Set boundaries based on your values. Knowing your truth helps you create relationships and environments that align with your well-being.
- Pursue personal goals with clarity. When you are honest about your strengths and passions, decision-making becomes easier.

- Engage in community healing efforts. Encourage collective truth-claiming in families, workplaces, and communities, creating safe spaces for dialogue and healing.

Truth fuels both self-liberation and communal empowerment.

The Freedom That Comes with Truth

Claiming your truths is one of the bravest things you can do. It means stepping out of denial, rejecting imposed identities, and embracing the fullness of who you are. It is a journey of self-discovery, healing, and empowerment, one that leads to greater confidence, clarity, and freedom.

For those impacted by PTSS and generational trauma, truth-telling is especially transformative. It allows for the release of inherited burdens, the reclaiming of cultural identity, and the building of a future rooted in self-determination.

Change does not happen by avoiding the truth. It happens by owning it, sharing it, and using it as a foundation for a better tomorrow. The more people embrace their truths, the more powerful the movement toward healing, justice, and transformation becomes.

Your truth is your power. Claim it, and watch how your world begins to change.

Conclusion

Conclusion

The Journey Toward Healing and Liberation

The journey through Post-Traumatic Slave Syndrome (PTSS) is not just about understanding trauma, it is about breaking cycles, reclaiming identities, and building a future rooted in healing and empowerment. The struggles outlined in this book are real, but so are the solutions. Healing is possible, transformation is attainable, and liberation is within reach.

As we conclude this exploration, it is important to reflect on the key themes that have emerged: the psychological, biological, economic, and social impacts of generational trauma; the role of internalized oppression in shaping identity; and the necessity of reclaiming our narratives, prioritizing mental health, and utilizing both individual and collective strategies for healing.

This conclusion serves as a call to action, not just to acknowledge trauma but to actively engage in the process of recovery. It is an invitation to apply what has been learned, take tangible steps toward self-empowerment, and contribute to the healing of our communities.

Healing Begins with Awareness

Acknowledgment is the first step toward transformation.

Many individuals and communities impacted by PTSS have lived in survival mode for generations, often without fully recognizing the psychological weight they carry. We have inherited not just cultural traditions and familial bonds but also pain, fears, and patterns of coping that originated in the historical trauma of slavery and systemic oppression.

However, awareness disrupts cycles. Once we recognize the impact of generational trauma, we can begin to dismantle the unhealthy patterns that have persisted for centuries.

- We acknowledge that PTSS is real. It is not an abstract concept or an exaggeration; it is a documented, observable condition that affects families, individuals, and communities in profound ways.
- We recognize the symptoms within ourselves. Whether it manifests as chronic stress, anxiety, depression, self-doubt, or relationship struggles, we must name what we experience in order to address it.
- We confront the sources of our pain. This means revisiting history, not to dwell on suffering, but to gain a deeper understanding of where these patterns originate.

Awareness is a powerful antidote to ignorance. When we name the forces that shape us, we take the first step in reclaiming control over our destinies.

Break Free from Internalized Oppression

One of the most insidious effects of PTSS is internalized oppression, the belief in the inferiority of one's own people, culture, or worth due to the messages imposed by an oppressive system. Over generations, these beliefs can become ingrained, leading to self-sabotage, distrust within communities, and a subconscious reluctance to embrace one's full potential.

Healing from internalized oppression requires intentional reprogramming:

- Rejecting false narratives. Society has told us stories about our history, value, and capabilities that are not based in truth. It is time to rewrite those narratives and reclaim our rightful place as resilient, innovative, and powerful individuals.
- Embracing cultural pride. Learning about the rich history, achievements, and strengths of our ancestors fosters a sense of self-worth and identity. This includes recognizing the brilliance of African civilizations, the contributions of Black leaders, and the enduring spirit of resistance.
- Challenging self-limiting beliefs. Many of the barriers we face are mental as well as external. It is crucial to question thoughts of inadequacy, fear, or self-doubt and replace them with affirmations of confidence, resilience, and greatness.

By unlearning the conditioning of oppression, we reclaim our right to self-love, self-determination, and self-empowerment.

The Role of Mental and Emotional Healing

Healing is not a passive process, it requires work, commitment, and consistent effort. Mental and emotional health must be prioritized, not just for individual well-being but for the collective good of the community.

1. Seeking Therapy and Professional Support
2. Therapy is an essential tool in unpacking trauma, processing emotions, and developing healthy coping mechanisms. The stigma around therapy in many Black communities must be dismantled, seeking help is a powerful act of self-care and not a sign of weakness.
3. Practicing Self-Compassion
4. Many people affected by PTSS carry feelings of guilt, shame, or unworthiness. Learning to extend grace and kindness to oneself is essential in the healing journey.
5. Building Healthy Relationships
6. Healing cannot happen in isolation. Surrounding oneself with supportive, uplifting, and understanding individuals creates an environment where growth can flourish.
7. Engaging in Mindfulness and Stress Management
8. Practices such as meditation, journaling, yoga, deep breathing, and gratitude exercises help regulate

emotions and reduce stress, contributing to long-term healing.

When mental and emotional health is nurtured, clarity, confidence, and resilience emerge.

Economic Liberation and the Path to Financial Healing

PTSS is not just a psychological issue, it has economic implications that span generations. From slavery to segregation to systemic discrimination in employment and housing, Black communities have been historically denied opportunities for wealth-building. Financial trauma is real, and healing requires active efforts to build generational wealth.

Steps Toward Financial Empowerment:

- Educating ourselves on financial literacy. Understanding how money works, budgeting, investing, credit management, and wealth accumulation, is crucial for breaking the cycle of poverty.
- Supporting Black-owned businesses. Economic self-sufficiency strengthens communities and provides opportunities for collective financial growth.
- Developing a mindset of abundance. Shifting from a scarcity mindset (fear of never having enough) to an abundance mindset (belief in the ability to create wealth) is crucial.

Financial healing is an integral part of overcoming PTSS, as economic stability allows for greater access to resources, opportunities, and overall well-being.

Reclaim the Power of Community

Healing is not just an individual process, it is a collective endeavor. Historically, Black communities have thrived through unity, mutual support, and shared responsibility. The breakdown of these systems due to systemic oppression and internal division has weakened the foundation of collective progress.

Ways to Rebuild and Strengthen Community Bonds:

- Investing in communal spaces. Churches, cultural centers, and grassroots organizations play a vital role in fostering connection and resilience.
- Mentorship and education. Teaching younger generations about self-worth, history, and financial literacy ensures that healing continues beyond one generation.
- Advocating for systemic change. Pointing issues such as mass incarceration, police brutality, and disparities in education and healthcare requires collective action.

Community is a source of strength, identity, and healing. By rebuilding communal bonds, we create a foundation for sustained progress and empowerment.

A Final Call-to-Action

This book is not just a reflection on trauma, it is a blueprint for change. It is an invitation to take the knowledge and turn it into actionable steps that lead to true transformation.

- Commit to personal healing. Whether through therapy, self-reflection, or spiritual growth, make the decision to actively work on your well-being.
- Challenge harmful narratives. Whether in conversations, media, or education, speak truth and reject distortions of history.
- Invest in future generations. Teach children about their history, worth, and potential, equipping them with the tools they need to succeed.
- Take control of your financial future. Break cycles of economic trauma by making informed financial decisions and creating generational wealth.
- Be an advocate for change. Whether through activism, community service, or policy change, use your voice and influence to push for justice and equity.

Healing is possible. Change is within reach. The future is ours to reclaim.

Let this be the beginning of a new chapter, one where past pain is acknowledged but no longer dictates our future. We are more than our trauma. We are our resilience, our strength, our creativity, and our endless potential.

Now, let's move forward together.

www.ingramcontent.com/pod-product-compliance
Lightning Source LLC
LaVergne TN
LVHW050818061126
851857LV00012B/862
* 9 7 8 1 8 0 8 5 0 0 3 7 4 *